The Daily Telegraph

Understanding COMPANY ACCOUNTS

FOURTH EDITION

BOB ROTHENBERG • JOHN NEWMAN

KOGAN PAGE

First published in 1988 by Telegraph Publications,
Copyright © The Daily Telegraph/William Curtis Ltd 1988
Second edition 1991
Third edition 1993
Fourth edition 1995

Kogan Page Limited
120 Pentonville Road
London N1 9JN

© Blick Rothenberg 1991, 1993, 1995

British Library Cataloguing in Publication Data

A CIP record for this book is available from the British Library.

ISBN 0-7494-1622-X

Typeset by Saxon Graphics Ltd, Derby
Printed and bound in Great Britain by
Biddles Ltd, Guildford and King's Lynn

Contents

Foreword and Acknowledgements

Our practice at Blick Rothenberg brings us into contact with a wide range of people in the course of a working year: successful entrepreneurs, extremely capable professional managers, wealthy individuals with funds to invest in companies and high powered finance directors. Each needs to understand company accounts.

The first three groups have always found that process difficult, and many have leant heavily on their accountants and, where appropriate, their finance directors. Yet the latest jargon-filled accounting standards – mini books in themselves – have made even some finance directors blush, when trying to explain them to their managing directors.

We have almost reached the point where the message about the state of a company's financial affairs is hidden and lost by the jargon and the detail which accounts contain.

The object of this book is to cut through the jargon and bring out the message.

In writing it we have tried to avoid getting tied up in technicalities. Some of our accountant friends might take issue with points of detail. We have erred on the side of simplicity, where we have erred at all.

This fourth edition takes account of legislation and accounting standards in issue as at 31 January 1995.

We should like to express our thanks to our colleagues at Blick Rothenberg and especially to David Rothenberg, who read the typescript for the first edition and made invaluable comments, and Finlay Forbes, who provided much appreciated input on the latest accounting standards. Our thanks also to Pippa Rothenberg, who read – and helped us to improve – the first edition; to our editors for their expert guidance; and to Carole Anderson for her continuing hard work in word processing all four editions of the book. Such faults as remain are all our own.

Bob Rothenberg and John Newman
London, 31 January 1995

Introduction

This book is not written for accountants. It is not even written for aspiring accountants. It is written for managers and owners of businesses, the kind of people for whom accounts are produced. It will not teach you how to prepare accounts. Most accountants will tell you it took them long, tedious months of study and practice before they came to grips with their profession. Fortunately, though, you do not need to be able to play a piano to recognise a good tune.

Our intention is that having read this book you should be able to tell whether the message from a set of accounts is good or bad. You should be able to judge how well the management of the business is performing. You should understand the jargon used by professional accountants. (But apart from what is necessary for understanding this language, we will keep the use of 'accountant-speak' to a minimum.)

Double-entry accounting

All accounts are prepared on the basis of double-entry bookkeeping or accounting, a system which has successfully operated for several hundred years. Although we are not going to teach you double-entry bookkeeping, some familiarity with the term will be useful. It is not, however, necessary to learn double-entry book-keeping to understand accounts.

The essence of double-entry bookkeeping is that two entries are made for every transaction.

Example
You buy a word processor for £500, and pay cash for it. Your accountant or bookkeeper makes two entries in your books. First,

11

he adds £500 to your business assets, representing the amount paid by your business for the word processor now owned by it. Second, he reduces your cash balance by £500, the amount of cash spent in acquiring the asset.

Similarly, two entries will be made for each and every other financial transaction entered into by a business. One entry will be called a *debit* (in our case the asset – the word processor – now owned by the business). The other entry will be called a *credit* (in our case the reduction in the cash balance). The total value of debits should always equal the total value of credits. Your accountant can then inform you that 'the books balance'. If the books do not balance this will indicate that an error has been made in recording a transaction somewhere along the line.

Some 10 or 20 years ago, accountants spent many hours a month balancing the books, tracking down and correcting errors made earlier in the month. Today, despite the widespread use of computers in keeping accounting records, accountants still continue to spend many hours a month balancing the books. (The term books is still used even when the records are computer-based.) However, the fact that the books balance merely means that the arithmetic is right; it says nothing about the business results; it does not even mean that the accounts are necessarily accurate, as we shall see later.

A word of caution

Before moving on to discuss accounts in the next chapter, a word of caution is necessary. Accounts are only as good as the accounting records from which they are prepared. If the books do not balance then something is obviously wrong. Unfortunately, though, the reverse is not true. The fact that the books balance does not mean that everything is correct, not even when they balance to the penny.

If your accountant tells you that the books balance so everything must be all right, maintain an element of scepticism. There are a number of things that could still be wrong.

Suppose you had bought the word processor mentioned earlier

for £500 but your accountant mistakenly entered the sum in the books as £600. The word processor would be shown as a business asset costing £600; cash would be reduced by £600. Since the same sum would have been entered on both sides the books would still balance. But they would be wrong. Business assets would be overstated by £100 and the cash balance would be £100 short. The error would be discovered when someone counted the cash and found it to be £100 more than recorded in the books. If the accountant then went back and checked each entry in the books relating to cash, he would eventually find that the invoice for the word processor was for £500 whereas the entry in the books was for £600. He could then correct the entry. But can you imagine how much more difficult the task would be if the invoice for the purchase of the word processor had not been retained?

Taking another example, suppose that your accountant completely forgot to enter the word processor transaction. In such a case, business assets would be understated by £500, representing the cost of the word processor which the business actually owns, but the cash balance would be overstated by £500, since the £500 which had been spent would not have been recorded. Again, the books would balance. The error would be discovered when someone counted the cash. He would find £500 less in the cash box than recorded in the books. Everyone would know that something was wrong, but unless they could locate the lost invoice there would be little that they could do to put matters right. They could, of course, check all the business assets and then find that a word processor was not recorded in the books, but they would still have to go one step further to find out when the word processor was bought and how much it actually cost.

Such errors are known as errors of omission. They are particularly difficult to detect. This is why, when a businessman scans a set of accounts, he should not just look to see what is there: he should also keep his mind on what *ought* to be there but is not.

Inherent uncertainty in accounts

The errors discussed above are at least capable of being corrected to make the accounts 100 per cent right. There is a third possibility, however. Going back to our example, everybody knows that a word processor will last for more than one year. Everyone also knows that it will not last for ever. It would seem reasonable to charge its cost against profits over the period of years in which it will be used. This is done by spreading its cost as an expense (known as *depreciation*) over several accounting years.

Unfortunately, no one knows exactly how long the word processor will last or what its second-hand value will be, if anything, at the end of its life. One person might think that it would last five years and then be thrown on the junk heap. He would therefore write off its cost of £500 over five years at £100 per year. Someone else might think that it would last 10 years and still have a second-hand value of £50 at the end of that period. Such a person might write it off over 10 years at £45 per year (£500 – £50 = £450 ÷ 10). Who would be right? Maybe neither, and no one will know until the word processor is finally scrapped or sold. In the meantime, there is an unavoidable element of uncertainty.

There are usually anything from a dozen to a hundred or more elements of uncertainty in every set of accounts you see. The number depends on the complexity of the accounts. Not all the uncertainties are trivial; some can involve very large figures indeed.

What conclusions can we draw? Can we ignore accounts because we know that they can never be 100 per cent accurate? A tempting thought, perhaps, but that would be going too far. The fact that it is not possible to arrive at 100 per cent certainty in a set of accounts is no reason for not trying to get as near to that figure as one can. After all, the reason that we need accounts is because we want to get the best estimate of what is actually going on. We want to get as close to the truth as possible. So do not worry unduly about every last pound, accept that there is an element of uncertainty, and understand that some, but not all, of the figures in a set of accounts will be approximate.

By the time you reach the end of this book you will understand what to look out for, and what to look upon with scepticism. You will have a feeling for how to use accounts for your benefit.

CHAPTER 1

Accounts –
Basic Principles

The accounting records, or books, list in detail all of a company's financial transactions during a given period of time. The *accounts* summarise the transactions recorded in the books during that period and show the financial position at the end of it.

The essentials of a set of accounts are two documents: a *profit and loss account* and a *balance sheet*. The *profit and loss account* shows the year's sales and expenses with the difference between the two being the profit or loss made by the business. After deducting tax payable to the government and any dividends payable to the business's owners, the remainder of the profit will be added to profits retained in previous years and included in the balance sheet.

The *balance sheet* shows how the business stands at the end of the year: the cost or valuation of its business assets; the sums of money owed to it by customers; the sums of money which it in turn owes to third parties; and, finally, the amount which, in a sense, it owes to its owners – the money which they originally contributed as the business capital, plus the profits after tax subsequently earned by the business but not paid out to its owners. The balance sheet is a snapshot of the position at the close of business on the last day of the year.

When talking about a business's profits, some people make the mistake of using the term balance sheet when what they really mean is profit and loss account. They talk about the profit for the year shown by the balance sheet when, as we have seen, the *annual* profit is shown by the profit and loss account. The confusion is probably caused because the balance sheet includes *total* profits to date which have been retained inside the business and not paid out to the owners.

The profit and loss account and balance sheet will each be set out on a single page. Most accounts also include ten or twenty pages of notes which give further details.

Accounts may take the form of published accounts or internal accounts. *Published accounts* are available to, and may be used by, people outside a business. *Internal accounts* are generally only available to senior managers within a business.

Most published accounts include three other statements in addition to the profit and loss account and balance sheet. The first of these is the *cash flow statement*. The cash flow statement shows the cash which the business has generated from its operations, the way in which it has been spent and the amount of cash left over. We shall return to it in Chapter 11.

The other two statements are potentially confusing to a lay reader of accounts. Happily, there are few circumstances in which most readers need give them more than a cursory glance. They are called the *statement of total recognised gains and losses* and the *reconciliation of movements in shareholders' funds*. The statement of total recognised gains and losses includes gains and losses which have not passed through the profit and loss account. The reconciliation of movements in shareholders' funds reconciles shareholders' funds at the start of the year with shareholders' funds at the end of the year. We shall say more about them in Chapter 12.

The Companies Act

Published accounts are regulated by the Companies Act 1985, as amended by the Companies Act 1989. We shall refer to this legislation simply as 'The Companies Act'.

The Companies Act does not apply to internal accounts.

The Companies Act requires published accounts to show a true and fair view; to be produced in a standard format; to disclose certain specific financial information; and (for large companies) to state whether they comply with applicable accounting standards. The first and last of these requirements need some comment now. We shall look at the others in detail in later chapters.

True and fair

There is no legal definition of the phrase 'true and fair', so what exactly does it mean?

We suggest that accounts should be true in that:

- They should be in accordance with all the known facts.
- Figures which are capable of correct and precise measurement within the time-scale available should be so measured.

We would suggest that accounts should be fair in that:

- Those figures which are surrounded by inherent uncertainties and cannot by their nature be 100 per cent correct should represent honest attempts to get as near the truth as possible.
- The view given by the accounts should not be misleading.

Overall, the accounts should give a balanced impression of a business.

Accounting standards

It is accepted amongst accountants that accounts have to be drawn up in accordance with *accounting standards* in order to give a true and fair view.

Accounting standards are a codification of many of the generally accepted accounting principles and conventions of the day. They were first drawn up by the *Accounting Standards Committee* and were known as *Statements of Standard Accounting Practice* or *SSAPs* for short. The Accounting Standards Committee was succeeded by the *Accounting Standards Board* whose pronouncements are termed *Financial Reporting Standards* or *FRSs*. Together, SSAPs and FRSs are known as accounting standards.

Qualified accountants have little choice but to follow accounting standards when drawing up accounts – or to be prepared to justify any departures from them to the *Review Panel*, which investigates cases where accounting standards have not been followed.

You may also come across the acronym *GAAP*, which stands for *Generally Accepted Accounting Practice*. GAAP embraces accounting practices followed by the majority of companies, whether or not they are the subject of accounting standards.

International accounting standards also exist but, to be honest, have little impact on most businesses in the UK, as they are either covered by UK accounting standards or are ignored.

Fundamental accounting concepts

The most important accounting standard identifies four *fundamental accounting concepts*. These underlie all published accounts and they therefore need to be understood. They have such general acceptance that you should assume they have been followed unless something to the contrary is said. The statement of directors' responsibilities, which is now attached to accounts (see Chapter 14), highlights the use of three of the concepts, but that is the only place where they are mentioned in accounts.

The first is the *consistency* concept. This says no more than that like items are to be treated consistently from one accounting period to the next. The other three concepts are the *accruals* concept, the *prudence* concept and the *going concern* concept.

The *accruals concept* states that income and costs are accounted for in the period to which they relate, rather than the period in which they are received or paid. Accordingly, if a sale is made on credit terms, it is recorded as a sale when it is invoiced, not when the cash is received. Similarly, an expense invoice is accounted for according to the date on which the expense was incurred, not the date on which the invoice was received or paid.

The accruals concept is sometimes called the *matching principle* since it also says that income and costs should always be matched to each other. If they were not so matched then the true profit and loss made on any transaction would not be shown. (Curiously, the accruals concept is the odd one out that is not mentioned in the statement of directors' responsibilities.)

The *prudence concept* states that losses are recognised at the earliest possible opportunity, whilst profits are recognised only when they can be seen in the form of cash or near cash. Where the accruals concept and the prudence concept conflict, the latter prevails. This reflects the basic conservatism with which published profit and loss accounts are produced.

The final fundamental accounting concept is the *going concern concept*. Under this, it is assumed that a business will continue in operation for the foreseeable future without significantly curtailing the scale of its operation.

This is important because the figures for assets in the balance sheet are *not* meant to represent what each asset could be sold for. The proceeds from a forced sale might be more than the figure in the balance sheet; but they are likely to be less. And if a business were to be closed, additional liabilities would almost certainly be incurred, such as redundancy costs. Such costs are not provided for in accounts drawn up on a going concern basis.

It is important to keep this in mind when reviewing accounts. It is one of the reasons why shareholders in companies which go into liquidation often receive far less than they hoped for. Assets have to be sold quickly, often for quite small sums, and large additional costs are incurred as a result of the liquidation itself.

Accounting policies

Accounting standards require accounts to disclose the principal accounting policies which have been followed. In non-accountants' language, *accounting policies* are the methods used to account for transactions where more than one method is possible. They will be set out either as the first note to the accounts or on a separate page of their own. It is important to watch out for unusual accounting policies when reviewing accounts, since such policies can significantly affect the figures.

The first accounting policy will generally state the *accounting convention* under which the accounts have been prepared and whether they have been drawn up in accordance with applicable accounting standards. (Any departures from accounting standards should be explained and justified.) In practice, only two accounting conventions are available. Under the *historical cost convention*, the value at which assets are recorded in a balance sheet is based on what they originally cost.

Under the *modified historical cost convention*, certain business assets (usually properties) are included at a more up-to-date valuation, though it may not be today's value. An accounting policy used by a business which follows the modified historical cost convention will read roughly as follows:

'The accounts are prepared under the historical cost convention as modified to include the revaluation of freehold land and buildings and in accordance with applicable accounting standards'.

In theory, there is a third accounting convention called the *current cost convention*. Under this, assets are recorded at what it would currently cost to buy them, not at what they actually cost. Such accounts are often known as *CCA* accounts and the accounting profession made an attempt to bring them into general use a decade or more ago. They never gained widespread acceptance, however, and virtually no published accounts are prepared on this basis any longer. We shall not dwell on the subject.

Other accounting policies may cover:

- The basis of consolidation and the basis of accounting for associated undertakings (see Chapters 2 and 7).
- Basis of accounting for goodwill (see Chapter 7).
- Depreciation basis and rate (see Chapter 7).
- Deferred taxation (see Chapter 3).
- Valuation of stocks and work in progress (see Chapter 8).
- Treatment of transactions in foreign currency (see Chapters 8 and 9).
- Basis of turnover figure (see Chapter 3).
- Leasing transactions (see Chapter 7).
- Pension costs (see Chapter 5).
- Treatment of research and development (see Chapter 7).

Directors and auditors

Accounts represent the directors' account of the financial performance of the business under their stewardship. One of the directors signs them as confirmation that all the directors agree the figures. Accounts include a specific acknowledgement by the directors that they take full responsibility for them. Before being published, however, accounts have to be examined by an independent firm of auditors. We discuss auditors further in Chapter 14.

Directors' report

The Companies Act requires the directors to write a narrative report to accompany the published accounts. This includes comparatively subjective items, such as a review by the directors of the development of the business during the year, and the directors' view of likely future developments.

This report is not audited, but if what it says is inconsistent with the accounts, the auditors have to say so.

Quoted companies, and some others, also include a chairman's statement which expands on the same topics. We discuss directors' reports and chairmen's statements in Chapter 13.

Where and how to find published accounts

If you are a shareholder in a company, the law requires it to send you a copy of its audited accounts and directors' report each year.

The Stock Exchange imposes certain additional requirements on quoted companies. Such companies are required to send annual audited accounts to shareholders within six months of the end of the accounting period; most send them within four months or so. They are also required to show additional information in annual accounts, such as earnings per share, and to send simplified half-yearly or quarterly accounts.

Perversely enough, though, the government introduced a provision a few years ago allowing listed public companies to send their shareholders *summary financial statements* in lieu of the proper accounts and directors' report. Any shareholder who wants to receive the full accounts and directors' report is still entitled to insist on them, however. We recommend that all shareholders should so do.

As well as being distributed to shareholders, the accounts of limited companies also have to be placed on public record. This is known as *filing* them and is done, for English and Welsh companies, at the Companies Registration Office in Cardiff. Copies of what is on record at Cardiff are kept at Companies House in London. In the case of Scottish companies, the accounts are filed in Edinburgh. Private companies' accounts have to be filed within ten months of the end of the accounting period which they cover (public companies have seven months). For companies with overseas interests these periods are extended by three months.

Companies registered in Northern Ireland, which are regulated by a separate Companies Act, must file their accounts in Belfast.

Any member of the public may inspect these records and obtain a microfiche copy of what is on file. There are a number of specialised agencies which will carry out a company search on your behalf. Their fees range from about £10 upwards, depending on the information you require.

We referred to public and private companies a little earlier. Many people are confused by the difference between a *public company* and a *private company*. In essence, any company can be a public company if it declares itself to be so and if it complies with certain not very onerous conditions laid down in the Companies Act. The main condition is that a public company must have a minimum allotted share capital of £50,000, at least 25 per cent of which must be paid up. It does *not* have to be quoted on the Stock Exchange and indeed may well be privately owned and not particularly large.

A public company will have the letters 'plc' (standing for public limited company) at the end of its name. The letters may be written in capitals and possibly with full stops.

A private company is simply any company which does not declare itself to be a public company. A private company will have the word 'Limited' (often abbreviated to Ltd) as the last word of its name.

Abbreviated accounts

Small and medium-sized private companies are permitted to file special accounts, known as *abbreviated accounts*, with the Registrar of Companies instead of normal accounts. Medium-sized companies still have to send normal accounts to their shareholders, but, since the end of 1992, small companies have been exempted from disclosing certain information to their shareholders. The accounts which shareholders in small companies get are now slightly less detailed than is the case for other companies.

Small companies

Abbreviated accounts for small companies are very abbreviated indeed. They consist only of a basic balance sheet, the amount of detail on which is very much restricted, and a few other items of information. Neither a profit and loss account nor a directors' report is included. If you look up the accounts of a company and all you find are the abbreviated accounts for a small company, you will be very little the wiser!

A small company is one which can meet at least two of the following three conditions:

1. Sales of not more than £2.8 million.
2. Total assets before deducting liabilities of not more than £1.4 million.
3. No more than 50 employees.

If you are a director of a company in this size category and you want as little financial information as possible to be placed on public record, you should ensure that abbreviated accounts are filed.

Medium-sized companies

In the abbreviated accounts of medium-sized companies, the amount of information shown on the profit and loss account is slightly condensed but, other than that, all other details required in normal accounts are included.

In order to qualify as medium-sized, a company has to satisfy at least two of the following three conditions:

1. Sales of not more than £11.2 million.
2. Total assets before deducting liabilities of not more than £5.6 million.
3. No more than 250 employees.

Banking, insurance and shipping companies

Banking, insurance and shipping companies are exempt from many of the rules and disclosure requirements applicable to other companies. Instead, they are subject to specialised requirements. These special cases are outside the scope of this book.

Internal accounts

Accounts which are published, sent to shareholders and made available to the general public will be true and fair and will comply with all the requirements applicable to them. They will, however, rarely give information over and above the minimum required, although there is nothing to prevent them from so doing. Taking into account all the supporting notes, the balance sheet will be fairly comprehensive. However, the profit and loss account will be less so. The amount of detail will be very limited. Among accountants, the published profit and loss account is often referred to as the *statutory profit and loss account* since its published form arises solely from statutory requirements.

For internal use, many companies will often attach a more comprehensive profit and loss account, known as a *detailed profit and loss account*, to the back of the accounts, inserting a note in front of it which says something to the effect that 'the pages which follow are only for the information of the directors and do not form part of the statutory accounts'. Bank managers and tax inspectors will always require sight of detailed profit and loss accounts – and to that extent will see more information about a company than a shareholder. Those details contained in the detailed profit and loss account which do not appear in the statutory profit and loss account are not audited.

The detailed profit and loss accounts are a form of *financial accounts*.

These annual profit and loss accounts are hardly sufficient, however, to enable management to run the business on a day-to-day basis. For this they will need more regular and more detailed internal accounts produced with their specific needs in mind. Internal accounts do not have to be audited and do not, by their nature, have to comply with any legislative requirements. Such internal accounts are usually referred to as *management accounts*, which means that they are produced for the purpose of assisting management in doing its job.

Management accounts and financial accounts

What are the differences between financial accounts and management accounts?

In their purest form, financial accounts are merely descriptive. They will describe each item of expenditure in the profit and loss account by its nature, usually adding similar items of expenditure together. All wages expenditure will be put together under the single category of wages. All rent paid will be shown as one figure.

Management accounts will provide a more detailed breakdown of individual items of income and expenditure. Sales income might be split between different products, or different regions, or both. Wages might be broken down by function: production workers, sales force, management and administration, for example. Rent might be charged to different departments: factory, selling and distribution department, management and administration might again be examples. The possibilities are endless. Management accounts can – and should – look very different in different industries, or between different businesses in the same industry. It should be possible for a manager to obtain information on the profitability or costs associated with any specified department, product or region.

The manager's job is sometimes defined as planning, decision-making and controlling. He should therefore ensure that his management accounts provide him with the information which he needs to help him carry out each of these tasks. The Institute of Internal Auditors have recently been quoted as saying that an extraordinary 70 per cent of internal management information is either not timely, nor relevant or not immediately understandable. It is up to the manager to make sure that the accounts presented to him do not fall into any of those categories!

Reconciling internal accounts and published audited accounts

At the end of the financial year it will be necessary to reconcile the profit shown by unaudited, internal management accounts to the profit shown by the published audited accounts. Management should make sure that they understand the reason for each significant reconciling item.

Some differences between figures in published accounts and figures in internal accounts are inevitable. Partly, this will be a question of time constraints. If internal accounts are to be produced quickly – and time is usually of the essence – then some accuracy will have to be sacrificed to timeliness. The more quickly the accounts are put together, the greater the number of estimates which they will contain. Partly, it will be a question of the two sets of accounts being produced using different assumptions. Many companies would not have the resources to calculate stock levels on a month-to-month basis with the degree of accuracy which would be required in the year end accounts; instead, they might use some form of approximation for the purposes of the monthly management accounts. Others might base the charge for cost of sales on what it would cost to *replace* the stock used, which would be more than the original cost if there had been a price rise, rather than on the *original* cost of the stock used.

Some might also base the depreciation charge on what it would cost to buy a replacement asset rather than on the original cost of the existing asset.

A company which was a member of a group might know that it would have to pay a management charge to another group company, but might not know what the exact charge would be until after the year end and so would have to use an estimate in its monthly internal accounts.

Finally, elements of the internal accounts might plainly and simply be wrong. It does happen, so read the accounts very closely. If a figure is not what you think it should be or does not seem to make sense, then query it. Ask for a breakdown. Find out what business transactions the figure is supposed to represent. If the accounts do turn out to be incorrect then find out why the mistake occurred and what corrective action needs to be taken to ensure that it does not happen again. Any decisions taken on the basis of incorrect information should be reviewed.

Before reading accounts

Before reading a set of accounts, whether they be published accounts or internal accounts, ask yourself a few questions. 'What am I going to decide, if anything, on the basis of reading these accounts? What information do I therefore need, when do I need it, and how precise does it have to be to assist me in making those decisions?'

When looking at internal accounts, ask yourself: 'What information will I subsequently need to enable me to monitor the implementation of any decisions which I may take on the basis of these accounts? What information do I need now to be able to monitor the implementation of decisions taken in the past?'

Decide to which area of the accounts you are going to give your attention and, if you are in the happy position of being able to obtain it, what additional one-off information you might need. It is easy otherwise to get lost in a mass of figures or to waste time on aspects of accounts which are irrelevant to one's real needs.

Key points

There is a great deal of truth in the saying that the key points, the points relevant to immediate decision-taking needs, or the key figures which put all the other figures in perspective, can be written on a single page. Try to get your company accountant to do this for you. Ask him to summarise other salient features of the accounts and to highlight any significant or unusual points. Such a practice will reinforce and strengthen the company accountant's sense of involvement as part of the team.

It should also reduce the likelihood of any significant points being missed.

Non-financial criteria

Although the information to be found in accounts is necessary in all areas of business you should not get *too* carried away. Financial criteria are not the *only* basis for decision taking, especially in the long term. A highly trained workforce and management team which is able to react quickly and successfully to unexpected events is also not without importance! Staff morale, corporate identity and brand image are almost always highly significant, but their achievement is difficult to measure in financial terms even though they will affect financial performance. The costs incurred in trying to achieve them can always be measured, however. Like all other costs, such costs need to be controlled, but achieving low costs in these areas as an objective in itself can be counterproductive if by so doing the whole point of the expenditure is overridden.

CHAPTER 2

Group Accounts

Many businesses are organised these days as groups of interlocking companies, one of which is the master company, or *parent company*, which owns or controls all of the others, known as its *subsidiary companies*. A group of companies might be organised in such a way that one company, call it Infallible Limited, owns 100 per cent of two other companies, Bertie Limited and Cecil Limited, with Bertie Limited in turn owning 75 per cent of Dellboy Limited. These three companies constitute a *group*, the group structure being as follows:

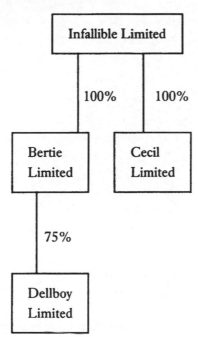

Figure 2.1 *Company ownership structure*

29

Each company will prepare its own accounts, but Infallible Limited will also prepare group accounts for the group as a whole. Group accounts will show the total results and total net assets of all the companies owned or otherwise controlled by Infallible Limited in proportion to its ownership of them. They are often called *consolidated* accounts. We shall use examples taken from the consolidated accounts of the Infallible group throughout this book (see Appendix on page 152).

If group companies are not owned 100 per cent by the parent company (either directly or through another subsidiary or subsidiaries) the proportion of the year's profit which is not 'owned' by the parent company will be deducted in the consolidated profit and loss account, and described as *minority interests*. Likewise, the proportion of the group's assets not 'owned' by the parent company will be shown as *minority interests* in the consolidated balance sheet.

Group accounts will also include the individual balance sheet of the parent company but *not* the parent company's own individual profit and loss account, cash flow statement, statement of total recognised gains and losses or reconciliation of movements in shareholders' funds.

Legal definition

Company law uses the term *subsidiary undertaking* rather than subsidiary company. The term embraces partnerships and unincorporated associations in addition to companies. Essentially, an undertaking will be a subsidiary undertaking where a parent company holds more than 50 per cent of the voting rights or, if not, controls its activities in some other way.

There is a precise legal definition. A subsidiary undertaking is one in which the parent either:

● has a majority of the voting rights; or
● is a shareholder and can appoint or remove a majority of the board of directors; or
● has the right to exercise a dominant influence through the subsidiary's Memorandum & Articles of Association (its basic constitution) or through a control contract; or

● is a shareholder and, by agreement with other shareholders, controls a majority of the voting rights; or

● has what is called a *participating interest* and either actually exercises a dominant influence or manages both itself and the subsidiary undertaking on a unified basis.

A *participating interest* is one held by a parent in a subsidiary on a long-term basis for the purpose of securing a contribution to its own activities by the exercise of control or influence. (A shareholding of 20 per cent or more is presumed to be a participating interest unless the contrary is shown).

What is the reason for the complexity of the definition?

A few years ago, there were a great many fancy schemes to dress up group balance sheets by the use of 'controlled non-subsidiaries'. These were companies which were safely in the parent company's control but structured so as to fall outside the previous Companies Act definition of a subsidiary, and which could therefore be excluded from group accounts. The parent would stuff the subsidiary full with bank borrowings and other liabilities, which in turn would be excluded from the group's balance sheet. The group's balance sheet would then look stronger. We discussed the mechanics of such schemes in the first edition of this book.

The current definition was designed to put a stop to such subterfuge. By including phrases such as 'dominant influence' it has, unfortunately, introduced a large element of subjectivity.

Even more subjectivity has been introduced by one of the latest accounting standards, *FRS 5 – Reporting the Substance of Transactions*. In essence this says that where an undertaking escapes the precise legal definition of a subsidiary while still being, in effect, controlled by the parent, it should be termed a *quasi subsidiary* and treated in the same way as if it was a legal subsidiary. (There is an exception where the quasi subsidiary in question has been used by the group to finance the purchase of a specific asset and meets the requirements for *linked presentations* – see page 95.)

Virtually every quoted company is a parent company, so almost all accounts published by quoted companies are consolidated accounts. Group accounts will show the name of each principal subsidiary undertaking and quasi subsidiary undertaking together with the nature of its business. They will also show the proportion of its share capital of each which the parent company owns.

Each subsidiary company still has to publish its own individual accounts in the same way as any independent company, even though it is part of a larger group. Its individual accounts will show the name of its ultimate parent company. The *ultimate parent company* is the parent company at the top of the pyramid of group companies. In Figure 2.1 (page 29) Infallible Limited would be Dellboy's ultimate parent company, although Bertie Limited would be its immediate parent company.

Associated undertakings

Group accounts may also include the results of associated undertakings. An associated undertaking is an undertaking which is not a subsidiary or quasi subsidiary but in which the parent has a participating interest (see page 31) and over whose operating and financial policy the parent exercises a significant, rather than dominant, influence.

The group's consolidated profit and loss account will show its share of the profits of all associated undertakings for the year, although the assets will not be taken up in the consolidated balance sheet. The group balance sheet will merely show the cost of the original investment in the associated undertaking plus the group's share of the associate's subsequent profits. The names of associated undertakings are shown as a note to the accounts.

Exceptions

Small and medium-sized groups do not have to prepare group accounts.

In order to qualify for this exemption, a group has to satisfy at least two of the following three conditions:

● Gross sales before consolidation adjustments of not more than £13,440,000 (or £11,200,000 after consolidation adjustments).

- Total assets before consolidation adjustments and before deducting liabilities of not more than £6,720,000 (or £5,600,000 after consolidation adjustments).
- No more than 250 employees.

Consolidation adjustments are the technical adjustments which accountants make to group accounts in order to eliminate transactions between group companies.

Where advantage is taken of this exemption, not only can the parent company avoid filing group accounts with the Registrar of Companies, it can also avoid sending them to its own shareholders. Such shareholders will therefore only see a partial picture of the group's activities.

CHAPTER 3

Profit and Loss Accounts – Format 1

We are now in a position to look at profit and loss accounts in detail.

First, we shall look at published statutory profit and loss accounts. These are laid out in one of two standard formats, called format 1 and format 2. Format 1 is by far the more common and is dealt with in this chapter. Chapter 4 will look at format 2 accounts. Chapter 5 will cover additional profit and loss account information and will illustrate a form of management accounts.

We shall show how to interpret the figures, and will look at some of the more important accounts ratios as we go along. We shall also comment on how management accounts might expand the information shown in published accounts or present it in a different manner.

We said that accounts have to be produced in one of two standard formats. That, at least, is what the Companies Act says. In reality, with the introduction of new accounting standards which bring in new accounting requirements, the format of accounts and the words used to describe the various items in the accounts are becoming less and less standard. As a consequence, certain information is becoming more difficult to find. No one seems to mind.

The Infallible group's consolidated profit and loss account, which is produced under format 1, is set out in Table 3.1. All its figures are shown in thousands of pounds. Smaller companies show their figures to the nearest pound; larger companies show them in millions of pounds. The same format of profit and loss account is used for both individual companies and groups. We shall first make some general comments about the huge mass of figures with which we are confronted and then look at each line in turn.

Table 3.1 *Consolidated profit and loss account for the year ended 31st December 1994*

	Notes	1994 £000	1994 £000	1993 £000
TURNOVER				
Continuing operations				
ongoing		15,508		14,505
acquisitions		2,403		–
		17,911		14,505
Discontinued operations		1,147		2,367
	2		19,058	16,872
Cost of sales	3		6,729	6,320
Gross profit			12,329	10,552
Net operating expenses	3		10,094	9,218
OPERATING PROFIT				
Continuing operations				
ongoing		2,331		1,361
acquisitions		2		–
		2,333		1,361
Discontinued operations		(98)		(27)
			2,235	1,334
Provision for loss on operations to be discontinued		–		70
Loss on termination of discontinued operations	4	86		–
Less: 1993 provision		70		–
			16	70
PROFIT ON ORDINARY ACTIVITIES BEFORE INTEREST			2,219	1,264
Interest payable less receivable	5		144	243
PROFIT ON ORDINARY ACTIVITIES BEFORE TAXATION			2,075	1,021
Tax on profit on ordinary activities	7		712	361
PROFIT ON ORDINARY ACTIVITIES AFTER TAXATION			1,363	660
Minority equity interests			5	3
PROFIT FOR THE FINANCIAL YEAR			1,358	657
Dividends	8		125	75
RETAINED PROFIT			1,233	582

The first two columns in the profit and loss account show the figures for the current year; the third column shows the figures for the previous year, as a means of comparison.

Continuing and discontinued operations

As a direct result of *FRS 3 – Reporting Financial Performance*, a fairly recent and quite radical accounting standard, the figures are analysed at various points in the profit and loss account between:

- the results of ongoing *continuing operations*
- the results of businesses acquired during the year – *acquisitions* – which are intended to be part of future continuing operations; and
- the results of businesses since sold or otherwise discontinued – *discontinued operations*.

When FRS 3 was written it had in mind those large groups which are constantly buying and selling businesses, opening them up and closing them down. Its aim was to allow users of accounts to see what sales and profits came from businesses forming part of a group's continuing operations; what sales and profits came from businesses sold or closed down during the year, or just after it; and what sales and profits came from businesses acquired during the year.

This seems fine in theory, and especially useful for professional analysts who spend hours examining accounts. Just what sort of valid conclusions they can draw in the cases of conglomerates, which have significant figures in each of the three columns year in and year out is perhaps less clear.

When FRS 3 came to define a 'discontinued activity' it hit a problem. Obviously, 'discontinued' includes the selling off or closing down of a major part of a business. Under FRS 3, it can also include a fundamental change in the market position of a business. If a fast-food chain changed to become a chain of high-class restaurants, such a move could well count as the discontinuation of a fast-food business and the start of a new trade (high-class restaurants). A move from owning a chain of shoe shops in Great Britain to owning a chain in America could be seen as discontinuing the British market and acquiring a new market in the USA. What about a move from England to Scotland? Would that also count as discontinuing one business and acquiring another?

There is clearly scope for some very subjective judgements to be made. This is particularly so in cases where there is a material and permanent reduction in the scale of a trade ('downsizing', in current jargon). FRS 3 views this as a discontinuation of part of a trade.

We could write several more pages on such points, but what we have said so far should be enough to convince you of the need to be sceptical.

The comparative figure for the previous year – 1993, in Infallible's case – will include only the results from the items in the current year's continuing activities column.

One final point needs to be made regarding the analysis of the year's results between discontinued operations, continuing operations and acquisitions during the year. There is an alternative form of presentation – a columnar form – which in some ways is superior to the form which the Infallible group follows. Unfortunately, few companies use it. The reason for its lack of popularity is probably a very simple one: it is harder to produce typographically, since it has more columns than the other method.

If the Infallible group had used the columnar form of presentation, its profit and loss account would have been presented as shown overleaf.

Turnover

The turnover of a company is the sales it makes to customers for the provision of goods and services, net of value added tax (VAT) and any applicable trade discounts. If you are looking at the consolidated accounts of a group of companies then the turnover shown will be for sales to customers outside the group. It is likely that some companies within the group will have sold goods and services to each other but such sales will have been eliminated

Table 3.2 *Consolidated profit and loss account for the year ended 31 December 1994 – Alternative Presentation*

	Continuing operations		Discontinued operations	Total	Total
	Ongoing	Acquisition			
	1994	1994	1994	1994	1993
	£000	£000	£000	£000	£000
TURNOVER	15,508	2,403	1,147	19,058	16,872
Cost of sales	5,034	1,118	577	6,729	6,320
Gross profit	10,474	1,285	570	12,329	10,552
Net operating expenses	8,143	1,283	668	10,094	9,218
OPERATING PROFIT	2,331	2	(98)	2,235	1,334
Provision for loss on operations to be discontinued					(70)
Loss on termination of discontinued operations			(86)	(86)	–
Less: 1993 provision			70	70	–
PROFIT ON ORDINARY ACTIVITIES BEFORE INTEREST	2,331	2	(114)	2,219	1,264
Interest payable less receivable				144	243
PROFIT ON ORDINARY ACTIVITIES BEFORE TAXATION				2,075	1,021
Tax on profit on ordinary activities				712	361
PROFIT ON ORDINARY ACTIVITIES AFTER TAXATION				1,363	660
Minority equity interests				5	3
PROFIT FOR THE FINANCIAL YEAR				1,358	657
Dividends				125	75
RETAINED PROFIT				1,233	582

from the consolidated accounts. The exact basis of arriving at turnover will be set out in one of the accounting policy notes.

The Infallible group's accounting policy, set out in Note 1 (k), is as follows:

'Turnover represents the invoiced value of goods sold, excluding sales between group companies, value added tax and trade discounts.'

If a company or group has two or more substantially different classes of business then an analysis of turnover between those different classes of business will be shown as a note to the accounts. The note will also show the profit or loss before tax made by each different class.

Similarly, if a company supplies different geographical markets then it will provide an analysis of turnover between those markets. Many companies interpret this requirement fairly broadly. Areas such as the UK, Europe, North America, Asia, and the Rest of the World are widely used.

The Infallible group has only one class of business but two geographical markets. It shows a geographical analysis of turnover in Note 2, reproduced in Table 3.3 below.

Table 3.3 *Geographical analysis of turnover*

	1994 £000	1993 £000
United Kingdom	16,818	15,191
North America	2,240	1,681
	19,058	16,872

Public companies, and companies which are ten times bigger than the statutory definition of a medium-sized company (see Chapter 1), also disclose additional information about the different classes of business and geographical markets – or 'segments' as they are sometimes called. They show sales made between different segments of the same company or group ('inter-segment sales'), the profit or loss made in different geographical markets and the net assets attributable to each segment. They also show the geographical area *from* which products or services are supplied (in addition to the geographical market *to* which they are supplied) and segmental information about associated undertakings.

When you look at turnover, you will get your first indication of the size of the business. Is its turnover measured in millions of pounds, tens of millions, hundreds of millions, or even more? Second, you will see the relative importance of the different classes of business which it undertakes, both in terms of size and profitability. Third, you will see where the customers reside. Whether having a high proportion of UK, European or North American customers is good, bad or unimportant is for you to decide. It will depend upon which markets you think are growing and which are in decline, how competitive you think conditions are in different markets and whether you think likely future exchange rate movements will be adverse or favourable to the company. Fourth, you will see the split between continuing operations, businesses acquired in the period and discontinued operations.

A set of internal management accounts would give much more precise figures if you wanted them. You could have turnover broken down in terms of individual salesmen or sales managers, if this information would help you to run the business. You might want sales to major customers to be separately identified; or a separate analysis of sales to new customers; or a statement of customers lost, showing the sales made to them in the previous period. Similarly, the number and value of credit notes issued could be analysed, giving the reasons for the credits. You ought to decide what information you want at the start of the year so that sales can be properly coded and analysed as the books are written up.

Just as important, or more important, than the absolute figures are the *trends*. Indeed, trends should be examined for each item in the accounts. Compare this year's sales with last year's figures and with figures over the last four or five years. Is the business growing or contracting and does the trend vary between different classes of the company's business or between different geographical markets? Is growth or decline steady, or is it an up and down, unstable sort of business?

Reduce the absolute numbers in the accounts to *percentages*, which are usually easier to work with. Again, this is something which can be done for all items in the accounts. Look at what turnover was, say, five years ago, and see by what percentage it has grown each year since then. There is no need to bother with decimal points, at least in the first instance; it is better to round each percentage to the nearest whole number. Studies have shown that round figures between 1 and 100 have much more meaning for most people than figures calculated to five or six decimal points.

If you are looking at management accounts, then pinpoint fairly precisely where the variances in sales have arisen. *Variance* is the word used by accountants to describe the difference between the figure looked at and the figure with which it is being compared. The latter will usually be either the budgeted figure or the figure for the previous period.

If a variance has arisen, who is responsible for the class of business or the market concerned? Why has it happened? Has it happened because of changes in price or volume? Are there external factors: is it price cutting by a competitor, competing products, an import embargo? Or is someone within the company not performing as they should? Is the variance temporary: what is the state of the current order book? If current orders are very high, will additional funds be needed to finance the increased level of activity? We shall look at the effect of changes in turnover on working capital in Chapter 9.

Cost of sales

This can be viewed as being the bulk of a company's *variable costs*, ie those costs which vary with the volume of output because they are directly related to the end product of the business. These include direct materials, direct labour and production overheads. Cost of sales is arrived at after taking into account stocks still held at the end of the period; it therefore comprises the direct cost of those goods or services which have actually been sold. As with turnover, cost of sales, together with all other expenses in the profit and loss account, excludes VAT.

Infallible's accounts show an analysis of cost of sales (and other expenses) between continuing and discontinued activities in Note 3, reproduced in Table 3.4 below.

Table 3.4 *Cost of sales and net operating expenses*

	1994			1993		
	Continuing	Discontinued	Total	Continuing	Discontinued	Total
	£000	£000	£000	£000	£000	£000
Cost of sales	6,152	577	6,729	5,252	1,068	6,320
Net operating expenses:						
Distribution costs	4,073	417	4,490	3,440	704	4,144
Administrative expenses	5,375	251	5,626	4,452	622	5,074
Other operating income	(22)	–	(22)	–	–	–
	9,426	668	10,094	7,892	1,326	9,218

The total figure for continuing operations in 1994 includes the following amounts relating to acquisitions: cost of sales £1,118,000; distribution costs £351,000; administrative expenses £954,000; and other income £22,000.

Cost of sales is often not a very important figure in itself when compared to the next figure, gross profit.

Gross profit

Gross profit is turnover less cost of sales. For managers within a company where pricing decisions are made using a marginal cost method, the absolute size of this figure will be of overwhelming importance, at least in the short term.

For many people, though, the absolute size of the figure will be less important than the *gross profit percentage*. The gross profit percentage is gross profit expressed as a percentage of turnover.

Example
The Infallible group's turnover is £19,058,000, cost of sales is £6,729,000 and gross profit is £12,329,000. Therefore, the gross profit percentage, is 65 per cent, calculated as follows:

$$\frac{12,329,000}{19,058,000} \times 100 = 65\%$$

You should compare this gross profit percentage with the previous year's figure, which was 63 per cent; it has therefore increased by 2 per cent. We can analyse the Infallible group's 1994 overall gross profit further, by extracting information on turnover from the profit and loss account and information on cost of sales from Note 3 (Table 3.4). The following gross profit percentages are then revealed:

Continuing operations (excluding acquisitions) 68%
Acquisitions 53%
Discontinued operations 50%

It is easy to understand why the group disposed of the comparatively less profitable operations, but why did it acquire businesses with only a slightly better gross profit percentage? A question for the directors, perhaps.

But you would not have been in a position to ask that question if you had not known where to look in the accounts to dig out the relevant information. If the Infallible group had used the alternative form of profit and loss account presentation shown in Table 3.2 then the relevant figures would have been shown on the face of the profit and loss account and the task would have been easier.

Perhaps that is a reason why the form of presentation shown in Table 3.2 is not popular with directors.

Gross profits should be compared with prior years to see if a trend is emerging. A comparison with the norm for the industry, or with the gross profit percentages made by its competitors, can also prove instructive.

When making such comparisons caution is advisable. Not all companies play the game by exactly the same rules. Some will include items in cost of sales which others include lower down the profit and loss account under a heading such as distribution costs, or even administrative expenses.

Mark-up

In the retail trade, gross profit percentage is the corollary of mark-up. Gross profit percentage compares gross profit with turnover; mark-up compares gross profit with cost of sales.

Example

The Infallible group's overall gross profit is £12,329,000 and cost of sales is £6,729,000. The mark-up is 183 per cent calculated as follows:

$$\frac{12,329,000}{6,729,000} \times 100 = 183\%$$

Where the gross profit is less than 50 per cent and can be expressed as a simple fraction, the mark-up can also be expressed as a simple fraction. The mark-up fraction has a denominator which is one whole number lower than the denominator of the gross profit fraction. This is less complicated than it sounds, as will be seen from the following examples:

Examples

		£	
(a)	Turnover	100	
	Cost of sales	67	
	Gross profit	33	
	Gross profit fraction	$1/3$	(33 divided by 100)
	Mark-up	$1/2$	(33 divided by 67)
(b)	Turnover	100	
	Cost of sales	75	
	Gross profit	25	
	Gross profit fraction	$1/4$	(25 divided by 100)
	Mark-up	$1/3$	(25 divided by 75)

And so on.

When you are looking at management accounts, bear in mind that the accuracy of the figure for stock held at the balance sheet date will have a significant bearing on the accuracy of the gross profit percentage. If stock records are unreliable, stock has not been properly counted or the valuation basis is incorrect or slap-dash, the reported gross profit and hence the profit percentage will be distorted. Stock is discussed in Chapter 8.

Net operating expenses

This heading groups together *distribution costs* and *administrative expenses*, after deducting minor miscellaneous operating income. The detail for the Infallible group is shown in Note 3 to the accounts, reproduced in Table 3.4 (on page 42).

Distribution costs

Distribution costs are the expenses incurred in distributing a company's goods to its customers. Such costs will almost certainly include transport costs and may include the wages and salaries of staff working in the distribution department. Selling costs, such as the costs of running sales outlets, advertising, the salaries of staff working in the marketing and sales departments, and agents' commissions will also often be included.

Many privately owned companies seem to have taken the view that distribution costs only comprise direct transport costs. Once again, it pays to be wary when comparing published accounts of different companies.

You have a right, however, to expect the same company to be consistent over a period of time in its treatment of different categories of expenses so you can look at trends in distribution costs in the same way that you look at trends in turnover. Look also at distribution costs expressed as a percentage of turnover and compare the changes over a period of time. This is much more informative than looking at distribution costs as absolute figures in isolation.

Example

In the Infallible group, total distribution costs for continuing operations are £3,722,000 (£4,073,000 less £351,000 relating to acquisitions – see Table 3.4) and represent 24 per cent of turnover for ongoing operations (which is £15,508,000 – see the profit and loss account), calculated as follows:

$$\frac{3,722,000}{15,508,000} \times 100 = 24\%$$

The comparable figure for the previous year was 24 per cent, so nothing much has changed in this area.

When looking at management accounts, look at each individual item contained within distribution costs in turn. Look at the largest item first. This rule applies to all areas of accounts. We all know managers who spend 20 minutes discussing fluctuations in the smallest item in the accounts in painstaking detail, and then have only two minutes left to skim over the largest or most significant areas of the accounts.

Compare each item of distribution costs with its budget, with the previous period, with trends over the last few periods and with turnover. Try to relate it to other information which you hold. If you know that the company recently switched its business from a cheap carrier to a more reliable but more expensive carrier, do not be surprised if carriage costs increase.

Administrative expenses

In published accounts, administrative expenses will often be the dustbin for those expenses remaining after costs have been allocated to other categories. The directors will not want the shareholders to get the idea that they are spending a great deal of money purely in administration. Spending money on distribution sounds much more productive. Smaller private companies are usually less concerned and are often quite happy for this category of expenses to grow to gigantic proportions.

The Infallible group's total administrative expenses for ongoing continuing operations have decreased from £4,452,000 in 1993 to £4,421,000 in 1994 (£5,375,000 less £954,000 relating to acquisitions – see Table 3.4) which sounds like good news.

When looking at management accounts, follow the same procedure for each item of administrative expenses as you do for distribution costs, though bear in mind that most administrative expenses will not vary in line with turnover.

Management accounts will probably not have a separate section headed administrative expenses. The costs are more likely to be broken down over detailed headings or spread over different cost centres. The same principles apply, though.

The following pointers may be helpful when looking at particular expenses.

- *Advertising and exhibition expenses.* Have any campaigns been mounted to increase the next period's turnover? (When looking at this period's turnover, consider what campaigns were mounted in the previous period!)
- *Consultancy/subcontractors.* What new consultants have been taken on and what rates are they paid? This figure should also be looked at in conjunction with payroll costs as individuals are sometimes switched from one basis to another.
- *Insurance.* Has the cover been increased? Is the cover adequate?
- *Motor expenses.* Consider changes in the size of the car fleet.
- *Rent.* Does the profit and loss account charge reconcile to the levels of rent set out in the leases?
- *Payroll expenses.* Consider the numbers of joiners and leavers, the last general pay rise and the average amount paid to each employee multiplied by the number of employees.

For all such expenses, the general level of inflation over the period is often useful as a yardstick.

You should also consider whether any items are non-recurring because they arise from special circumstances in the current period. Looked at from another point of view, what special circumstances have there been which *ought* to have given rise to higher or lower expense levels? Have those expected expense levels been reflected in the profit and loss account?

Other operating income

Miscellaneous operating income is shown under this heading and is usually deducted from distribution costs and administrative expenses. It is a dumping ground for any income that is associated with a company's ordinary activities, but which does not fall under the definition of turnover and does not come within one of the other categories of income. In management accounts you would be provided with full details of any other operating income. Further details are sometimes given in published accounts.

Operating profit

At this point in the profit and loss account a line is drawn to show the operating profit made by the enterprise. This is the profit before any income or expenses specifically highlighted as being of an *exceptional* nature, and is also arrived at before charges for interest and tax.

Exceptional items

Before FRS 3, accountants distinguished between *exceptional* and *extraordinary* items. However, under the new accounting standard, *extraordinary items* have practically disappeared and there is therefore little point in giving their theoretical definition. The authors of the standard say that, while extraordinary items may exist, they are so rare that they cannot think of any examples! (We have a vision of a new science fiction film in which extraordinary items float around at the extremities of the galaxy, just out of reach, just out of sight . . .)

Back on earth, many transactions that used to be classified as extraordinary are now called *exceptional items*. An exceptional item is a material figure which needs to be disclosed separately, by virtue of its size or incidence, if the accounts are to give a true and fair view.

FRS 3 effectively recognises two separate classes of exceptional items: those which are defined as exceptional under paragraph 20 of the FRS; and the rest. 'Paragraph 20' items bear a striking resemblance to old-style extraordinary items. They are treated differently from other exceptional items in that they *must* be shown separately on the face of the profit and loss account immediately after operating profit. (Other exceptional items will usually be shown by way of a note; they should only be included on the face of the profit and loss account if such prominence is necessary to give a true and fair view.) The main 'paragraph 20' exceptional items are profits or losses on the sale or termination of an operation and the cost of a fundamental reorganisation or restructuring of a business.

The Infallible group has shown a loss on the termination of discontinued operations as an exceptional item just after the figure for operating profit. The notes to the accounts show the effect which the exceptional item has had on the taxation charge for the year. Where appropriate, the effect of exceptional items on minority interests is also shown.

Operational gearing ratio

We can now look at the relationship between operating profits and changes in turnover by looking at the operational gearing ratio. This ratio shows how sensitive operating profits are to increases or decreases in turnover.

The ratio is calculated as follows:

$$\frac{\text{Turnover} - \text{variable costs}}{\text{Operating profits}}$$

In the case of published format 1 profit and loss accounts, *variable costs* can usually be taken as cost of sales and distribution costs.

Example

The Infallible group's turnover for 1994 on continuing operations (including acquisitions) is £17,911,000; cost of sales is £6,152,000 and operating expenses are £9,426,000 including distribution costs of £4,073,000. The corresponding operating profit is £2,333,000 (£17,911,000 less £6,152,000 less £9,426,000). Its operational gearing is therefore 3.3, calculated as follows:

$$\frac{17,911,000 - (6,152,000 + 4,073,000)}{2,333,000} = 3.3$$

This means that a 20 per cent increase in turnover would lead to a 66 per cent increase in operating profits (20 per cent × 3.3), as shown below:

	£000	£000
Turnover		
(£17,911,000 + 20%)		21,493
Cost of sales		
(£6,152,000 + 20%)	7,382	
Distribution costs		
(£4,073,000 + 20%)	4,888	12,270
		9,223
Administrative expenses	5,375	
Other operating income	(22)	5,353
Trading profit		3,870

The new trading profit of £3,870,000 is 66 per cent higher than the original trading profit of £2,333,000. To have quite a high operational gearing ratio like this is good news when times are good and businesses are expanding. But it is decidedly bad news when sales fall. If the Infallible group's turnover were to fall by 20 per cent then its trading profit could be expected to fall by 66 per cent to just £793,000. So how you interpret this ratio – and how you interpret every financial ratio – depends upon your views on the wider context in which a company operates.

The comparable figure for the previous year was 4.3.

The Infallible group's 1994 sales (excluding acquisitions) increased by 15 per cent over 1993. With an operational gearing ratio of 4.3 for 1993 this should have led to an increase in operating profits (excluding acquisitions) of 65 per cent (15 per cent × 4.3). In fact, the corresponding figure for operating profits increased by 64 per cent, much in line with the prediction.

Nevertheless, we should always maintain an element of scepticism when interpreting accounts in this way. Things do not always work out so neatly! Variable costs might not change in direct proportion to turnover; we might have identified them incorrectly. Caution and scepticism should be your motto when looking at accounts. Nevertheless, a change in turnover of 20 per cent will clearly have very different results in a company with an operational gearing ratio of 3.3 compared with another company with a ratio of 1.3 and a third company with a ratio of 8.3.

Profit on ordinary activities before interest

At this point, a subtotal is drawn in the profit and loss account to show the *profit on ordinary activities before interest*. Let us call this *trading profit* for short.

A number of further calculations can be made. (If the Infallible group's profit included any profits of associated undertakings we would exclude them from the calculations.)

Profit margin on sales

Trading profit can be expressed simply as a percentage of turnover, as below:

$$\frac{\text{Trading profit}}{\text{Turnover}} \times 100$$

Example

The Infallible group made a trading profit of £2,219,000 on turnover of £19,058,000. Its overall trading margin is 12 per cent as shown below:

$$\frac{2,219,000}{19,058,000} \times 100 = 12\%$$

The comparable figure for the previous year was 7 per cent.

On its continuing operations (including acquisitions) however, the Infallible group's trading margin was 13 per cent, indicating, perhaps, an even better result for next year.

Different industries will make different profit margins on sales, so the precise margin made is mostly of significance for comparative purposes.

Trading profit and employee costs

If the figure for employee costs is known then trading profit can be expressed as a percentage of employee costs, as follows:

$$\frac{\text{Trading profit}}{\text{Employee costs}} \times 100$$

This will show the sensitivity of trading profit to pay rises and will be particularly significant in companies which provide services.

Example

A company's trading profit happens to be equivalent to its payroll. A 10 per cent increase in its payroll bill will lead to a 10 per cent decrease in trading profit, other things being equal.

A second company's trading profit is only 50 per cent of its total payroll bill. In its case, a 10 per cent increase in payroll costs will lead to a 20 per cent decrease in trading profit, ie its profitability is much more sensitive to pay rises.

Interest payable less receivable

Interest payable comprises interest paid to banks, hire-purchase companies and so on. You can compare interest payable with borrowings and market rates of interest.

Interest receivable is usually shown as a deduction from interest payable.

Details for the Infallible group are set out in Note 5 to the accounts.

Many people will be interested in how much of the company's profits are eaten up by interest charges. If the proportion is high, banks will know that just a small fall in profitability might cause the company to have difficulty in meeting its interest bill. A bank may be wary of lending to a company in that position. Creditors will probably feel the same way since a company which could not pay its interest bill would be a company in financial difficulties. Shareholders will also feel unhappy. *Interest cover* is the ratio which they all use to measure this point.

Interest cover

This shows the number of times that interest payable is covered by profits before tax and interest payable. Profits before tax and interest payable are often known as *earnings before interest and tax* or *EBIT*. Interest cover is calculated as follows:

$$\frac{\text{EBIT}}{\text{Interest payable}}$$

Example

The Infallible group made a profit on ordinary activities before interest and tax of £2,219,000. Net interest payable was £144,000. Its interest cover is very high at 15. This means that interest payable is covered 15 times by EBIT. The comparable figure for the previous year was 5.

Where interest cover is low, a small fall in EBIT might cause a company to have trouble in meeting its interest bill. Shareholders could be left with no earnings at all.

Profit on ordinary activities before taxation

Profit on ordinary activities before taxation will be the next heading in the profit and loss account.

Tax on profit on ordinary activities

The figure here will represent the total amount of tax which the business will have to pay on the profit it has made on its ordinary activities for the period. The figure is analysed, usually in a note to the accounts, between:

● UK Corporation Tax
● Deferred taxation
● UK Income Tax
● Overseas taxation
● Irrecoverable Advance Corporation Tax.

If you are looking at a consolidated profit and loss account which includes the appropriate share of the results of an associated undertaking, the equivalent share of the tax charge for that company will be separately identified.

United Kingdom Corporation Tax

United Kingdom Corporation Tax is the tax which companies have to pay to the UK Inland Revenue on their profits. The current rate is 33 per cent for profits over £1,500,000 and a lower, 'small company' rate of 25 per cent is paid if profits are less than £300,000. There is a sliding scale between those two amounts with profits between the two effectively taxed at 35 per cent!

Additional rules mean that companies which are members of groups or are under common control may start paying the full rate of tax at lower levels of profits.

The profit which a company shows in its accounts will rarely be the exact figure on which Corporation Tax is charged. This is because various adjustments are made to the stated profit for tax calculation purposes. The charge for UK Corporation Tax on profits of, say, £2 million will therefore rarely be exactly £660,000. The tax adjustments are not shown anywhere in the accounts so you cannot check the tax charge yourself.

Some of the adjustments are permanent. For instance, certain expenses, such as those incurred in entertaining customers, are not allowed as deductions for tax purposes. These have to be added back to the profit shown by the accounts before calculating the tax liability. Other adjustments are temporary.

Deferred taxation

Temporary adjustments can arise when items are dealt with for tax purposes in a different year from the year in which they are included in the accounts. When allowances are given for tax purposes earlier than expenditure is charged in the accounts, or where income is taxed in a later year than it is included in the accounts, taxation liabilities can be deferred from the current period to a later period. This is known as *deferred taxation*.

Accounts include a charge for deferred taxation so as to even out fluctuations in the tax charge caused by temporary timing differences. The charge covers amounts of tax which it is known have only been temporarily deferred and will eventually become payable. It can be looked on as an example of the accruals concept or matching principle – in this case, matching the tax charge with the accounting profits.

If you add the charges for UK Corporation Tax and for deferred taxation they will usually be much nearer the expected tax rate than the charge for UK Corporation Tax alone. Temporary timing differences will have been more or less eliminated, and only the permanent differences caused by the tax rules will remain.

United Kingdom Income Tax

In addition to Corporation Tax, a company will suffer UK Income Tax on any *franked investment income* which it receives. Franked investment income consists of dividends from UK companies. Associated with the receipt of a dividend is a tax credit covering the Income Tax due (see Advance Corporation Tax below).

Irrecoverable ACT

ACT stands for *Advance Corporation Tax*. This is the tax which a company has to pay to the Inland Revenue when it pays dividends to shareholders and currently amounts to one-quarter of the net dividend.

A company can, in most cases, set off ACT paid against the Corporation Tax it will pay on its profits for the year (known as *mainstream* Corporation Tax). Sometimes, though, the ACT will be greater than the tax rules allow to be offset. If there is no immediate prospect of its recovery it will be written off to the profit and loss account as irrecoverable ACT.

Special tax circumstances

Any special circumstances affecting the amount of tax which the company has to pay in the current or succeeding years will be disclosed in a note to the accounts.

Profit on ordinary activities after taxation

This is what is left of the profit after providing for all tax payable on it. It is sometimes known as *earnings* and is the figure which is used, after adjusting for minority interests, when calculating *earnings per share* and, for quoted companies, *the price earnings ratio*. Earnings per share is sometimes known as *EPS* and the price earnings ratio as the *PE ratio*.

Minority interests

Profit attributable to minority interests appears in group accounts only and represents that part of the profit of non wholly owned subsidiary companies which is 'owned' by outside shareholders and not the parent company. In the case of the Infallible group, the group owns only 75 per cent of the subsidiary company Dellboy Limited. The remaining 25 per cent is owned by outside shareholders. We may assume therefore that the profit of £5,000 attributable to minority shareholders represents 25 per cent of the post-tax profits made by Dellboy Limited.

The figure of £5,000 is further analysed between *equity* and *non equity* minority interests – a requirement of one of the latest accounting standards. The terms 'equity' and 'non equity' are discussed on page 115.

Earnings per share

Assuming that there are no preference shareholders, earnings per share is calculated as follows:

$$\frac{\text{Profit on ordinary activities after tax and minority interests}}{\text{Number of ordinary shares in issue}}$$

Quoted companies are required to disclose earnings per share on the face of the profit and loss account, so the calculation will be done for you.

Many quoted companies publish a second figure for earnings per share after eliminating the effect of exceptional items. They will sometimes describe this as the 'normalised' figure for earnings per share. It is perhaps not unduly cynical to predict that the eliminated items will mostly be losses! Nevertheless, quoted companies are *required* to publish the figure for earnings per share before any such eliminations.

You may sometimes see reference made in quoted companies' accounts to earnings per share calculated on a net basis and on a nil distribution basis. The *net basis* is the normal one and takes account of all taxation charges.

The *nil distribution basis* excludes from the tax charge any irrecoverable ACT or overseas tax suffered because of dividend payments or proposed dividends. The nil distribution basis is thought by some to make earnings per share slightly more comparable between different companies since EPS on this basis is not affected by differences in dividend policies. Where EPS calculated on a nil basis is significantly different from EPS calculated on the normal basis, both figures are disclosed. This happens most commonly when companies have large overseas tax charges, such as oil companies.

You may also see reference made to *fully diluted earnings*. This is relevant where, for one reason or another, additional shares are likely to rank for dividends in the future and will therefore dilute earnings per share at that point. Where such circumstances apply, the figure for what earnings per share would have been if such shares ranked for dividend today is also given. It is known as *fully diluted earnings per share*.

Look at the earnings per share over a period of time. Is the figure going up or down? If it is going down, is it because the business is becoming less profitable or because more shares have been issued and this has diluted the average earnings per share?

For the Infallible group, earnings per share are £27.16, calculated as follows:

$$\frac{£1,363,000 - £5,000}{50,000} = £27.16$$

The comparable figure for the previous year was £13.14.

Price earnings ratio

For quoted companies, the price earnings ratio is one of the most commonly used yardsticks for judging share prices and values. It shows how many years' earnings per share the share price represents, and is calculated as follows:

$$\frac{\text{Share price}}{\text{Earnings per share}}$$

The price earnings ratio will show how highly the company is rated by the stock market. If one company's shares are priced at 15 times its earnings and another company's priced at only 6, then this is likely to mean that the market rates the former company rather higher than the latter. But it might mean that the former company had just suffered a bad year and the market expects it to recover. Like any other figure, it has to be interpreted; the reader must put it into context and form his own opinion.

Profit for the financial year

This is the profit remaining for the year after all costs have been charged and all taxes provided.

Dividends

A business can either pay out profits as dividends to shareholders or it can retain them in the business.

The next line of the profit and loss account shows interim dividends which have been paid together with any final dividend recommended by the directors.

Dividend yield

Anyone who owns shares in a company and pays attention to the amount of income received from those shares will be interested in their *dividend yield* of the shares, compared with other available shares. Dividend yield is the gross dividend per share expressed as a percentage of the current share price. The *gross dividend* is the net dividend actually paid, plus the associated tax credit. If the figure for gross dividend is not readily available from the accounts it can be calculated easily by adding one-quarter to the net dividend. Dividend yield is based on gross dividend because this forms the basis of the taxable income in the hands of the recipient, who may have to pay higher rate tax.

The gross dividend yield is calculated as follows:

$$\frac{\text{Gross dividend in pence}}{\text{Share price in pence}} \times 100$$

Example

The net dividend is 12p; the gross dividend is therefore 15p, (12p + one-quarter); and the share price is 300p. Gross dividend yield is 5 per cent, calculated as follows:

$$\frac{15}{300} \times 100 = 5\%$$

Dividend yield can only be calculated when the current share price is known and is therefore mainly of significance for shareholders of quoted companies – and the managers of these companies who have to keep their shareholders happy. Nevertheless, there are circumstances when it can also be of importance to shareholders of unquoted companies, for instance on occasions when the value of those companies has to be negotiated with the Inland Revenue.

Dividend cover

Dividend cover is the number of times the dividend per share is covered by the earnings per share and is usually calculated based on the net dividend, as follows:

$$\frac{\text{Earnings per share}}{\text{Net dividend per share}}$$

Example
Earnings per share are 35p; net dividend per share is 12p. Dividend cover is 2.9:

$$\frac{35}{12} = 2.9$$

You should be aware that dividend cover becomes more complicated when a company has overseas earnings and suffers foreign tax. Since foreign tax cannot be set off against UK Corporation Tax, this complicates the amount of dividend which a company could pay out of its profits. The amount becomes restricted. In such cases, dividend cover is calculated on what is known as a *full distribution basis*, as follows:

$$\frac{\text{Full distribution EPS}}{\text{Actual gross dividend}}$$

The full distribution EPS is the maximum gross dividend the company could distribute without eating into its retained profits from earlier years. (How this figure is arrived at is beyond the scope of this book.)

Retained profit

Retained profit is the final line in the profit and loss account and shows the profit left over after all expenses, taxation and dividends.

CHAPTER 4

Profit and Loss Accounts – Format 2

Format 2 is the alternative form of presentation for published profit and loss accounts. If the Infallible group had presented its profit and loss account under format 2, the figures for the year ended 31 December 1994 would appear as set out in Table 4.1.

Table 4.1 *Profit and Loss Account – Format 2*

	1994 £000	1994 £000
TURNOVER		
Continuing operations		
ongoing	15,508	
acquisitions	2,403	
	17,911	
Discontinued operations	1,147	
		19,058
COSTS LESS OTHER INCOME		
Changes in stocks of finished goods and work in progress	(90)	
Raw materials and consumables	5,356	
Other external charges	6,374	
Staff costs (see Note 23)	4,540	
Depreciation of fixed assets	138	
Other operating charges	527	
Other operating income	(22)	
		16,823
OPERATING PROFIT		
Continuing operations		
ongoing	2,331	
acquisitions	2	
	2,333	
Discontinued operations	(98)	
		2,235

The presentation of the remaining part of the profit and loss account would be same as for format 1.

Format 2 breaks down expenditure by its type; format 1 broke it down by function. Format 2 is used more commonly by manufacturing companies, although even manufacturing companies divide fairly evenly between those who use format 1 and those who use format 2. Almost all other companies use format 1.

The two formats are similar in many ways (although the layout differs) and so we will consider here only those items which are unique to format 2.

Changes in stocks of finished goods and work in progress

This shows the movement between the current year's stock of finished goods and level of work in progress and the corresponding figures for the previous year. If this year's figure is higher than last year's, as is the case with the Infallible group, the difference will increase profits; if the reverse is true it will reduce profits.

Raw materials and consumables

This is the cost of raw materials and consumables after excluding the amount of stock still held at the end of the period.

Other external charges

This is a catch-all which includes items which do not fall under any of the other headings.

Staff costs

This is self-explanatory.

Depreciation

This, again, is self-explanatory.

Other operating charges

This, like other external charges, is a catch-all category. The split of expenses between the two headings can be arbitrary and comparisons between different companies are not, therefore, usually very illuminating.

Other headings

There are certain other minor headings in format 2 which do not apply to the Infallible group. They are generally self-explanatory apart from the heading of *Own work capitalised*.

This heading represents any costs which a company has incurred in manufacturing its own plant and machinery, constructing its own buildings, or otherwise building its own fixed assets. The costs incurred would have been charged under one or more of the other expense headings and so an item on this line will increase profits.

As with format 1, further detailed information, such as an analysis of expenses between ongoing continuing operations, acquisitions and discontinued operations, will be given in the notes to the accounts.

CHAPTER 5

Profit and Loss Accounts – Additional Information and Management Accounts

In addition to the figures on the face of the profit and loss account, additional information is given in the notes to published accounts. This will include, where applicable:

- Rent receivable
- Income from listed investments
- Cost of hiring or leasing plant and machinery
- Cost of leasing other assets
- Depreciation charge
- Audit fees (Companies which do not qualify as small or medium-sized (see Chapter 1) must also show the fees paid to their auditors for non-audit services, such as taxation advice or management consultancy)
- Net gains or losses in foreign currency borrowings, and whether charged to the profit and loss account or direct to reserves
- Directors' remuneration
- Average number of employees, analysed over appropriate categories, and the costs of employing them
- Particulars of pensions.

Most of these headings are self-explanatory, but a few are worthy of comment.

Directors' remuneration

Most people will show an interest in what the directors earn – especially if what they earn goes up each year, however well or badly their company does! Accounts will show the total figure for all the directors split between fees, management remuneration, pensions and compensation paid to past directors for loss of office. (This last requirement is why golden handshakes have to be disclosed.) The figures will include pension costs and the estimated money value of benefits in kind. Any sum paid indirectly to a director, such as sums paid to a company controlled by him for the provision of his services, are also included.

If total emoluments exceed £60,000, or if the company is a member of a group, the following (even more interesting) details are also shown:

- Chairman's emoluments
- Emoluments of the highest paid director, if higher than the chairman
- The number of directors whose emoluments (excluding pension costs) fall into each £5,000 bracket: from £0 to £5,000; £5,001 to £10,000; and so on
- If any directors waived emoluments, the number who waived them and the total waived. (Quoted companies also give details of waivers of future emoluments.)

In addition, quoted companies, and others which follow the recommendations of the Cadbury Report, will show how much of the total directors' remuneration arose from performance-related bonuses. This information will also be given for the chairman and the highest paid director individually.

Finally, since September 1994 a pronouncement from the *Urgent Issues Task Force* has meant that most large companies also show details of share options granted to, or exercised by, directors as part of the note on directors' remuneration. This disclosure is, however, not mandatory.

The Infallible group shows directors' remuneration in Note 22 to its accounts.

Where relevant, the accounts will also give details of any other significant transactions between the company and its directors. Group accounts will show such details in respect of directors of the parent company only.

Employee information

Details given about employees will include the average number employed during the year (analysed over appropriate categories) and the costs of employing them. It is therefore possible to calculate the costs attributable to each employee. Differences between companies in the same industry can be illuminating. The information is given in the Infallible group's accounts in Note 23.

Pension costs

Pension costs can have a very significant impact on a company's profits as the figures are often very large.

Although employees may make contributions into a company pension scheme, we are only concerned here with the treatment of an employer's contributions – the company's costs.

Most pension schemes are funded schemes. (A *funded scheme* is one where a company makes provision for future pensions by making payments into a separate fund administered by independent trustees. The idea is that once the employer has made a payment he has no further access to the money so that it cannot be misused. As recent events have shown, things do not always work out like that in the real world.) There are two different types of funded schemes: *defined benefit* schemes and *defined contribution* schemes. It is defined benefit schemes that cause accounting problems.

Defined benefit schemes

Most non-accountants know defined benefit schemes as *final salary* schemes. In such schemes, an employee's pension is based on his final salary and number of years' service. Therein lies a problem. The company cannot know how many years an employee will serve, nor the employee's final salary in 10, 20, 30, or perhaps 40 years' time. Consequently the company cannot calculate the exact pension it will have to pay in the future and therefore what provision it should be making for it now. Faced with this uncertainty, the company will pay money into a pension scheme and hope that the investments made by the scheme will grow enough to pay appropriate pensions to all its employees when they retire. The level of payments made into the scheme is based on advice from actuaries. Their advice is based on applying scientific principles to basic assumptions. The basic assumptions, frankly, are based on guesswork.

As time passes, the assumptions will prove to be either right or wrong. If they are wrong, the pension scheme assets will either be insufficient to match pension scheme members' accrued benefits, or pension scheme assets will be greater than necessary. The company will then either increase or decrease the level of its future payments into the scheme.

Despite these problems, accounting standards require a company to make a broadly non-fluctuating charge to its profit and loss account, year-in, year-out, whatever its current level of payment. (This assumes that there are no significant changes to the workforce or pension scheme.) The charge has to be the expected long-term *regular pension cost*. If the company pays more or less than this in a particular year, the difference is carried forward in the balance sheets as a prepayment or accrual. The idea is that changes to levels of payments caused solely by changes in assumptions (which we described earlier as guesswork) will not cause violent fluctuations in the profit and loss account charge.

Because the assumptions on which pension costs are based are so important, they have to be described in the accounts. The main assumptions will generally be those covering the growth of pension scheme investments, the rate of expected future salary increases (which will determine the expected final salaries on which pensions will be based) and future pension increases.

The accounts will also disclose the actuarial value of pension scheme assets as a percentage of the benefits which had accrued to members at the valuation date. Ideally, this will be 100 per cent at any given time. A few points above or below does not matter very much. If the difference is significant, however, the company will say what action it proposes to take.

Most of the information is usually disclosed in a note headed *'Pension Costs'*. Reference should also be made to the accounting policy, the employee information note (to see the pension costs for the year) and the notes on debtors and creditors to see whether the accounts contain any pension prepayments or accruals (for which see later chapters).

Pensions are a very long-term business. Whether accounts should really be looking 15 or 20 years ahead in this fashion is perhaps open to debate. So much can change in such an extended period. The authors are reminded of the economist John Maynard Keynes's remark: 'In the long run, we are all dead'.

The overriding importance which standard accounting treatment gives to preventing the pension cost charge in the profit and loss account from fluctuating when it is in the nature of things for it to do so may also be open to question.

In any event, readers of accounts will receive sufficient information to enable them to form their own views about the implications for a company of its own pension costs circumstances.

Defined contribution schemes

Under the second type of funded pension scheme, called a *defined contribution scheme*, an employer makes fixed payments into a pension fund and that is the end of the matter. The pensions which employees eventually receive are based entirely on how well the pension scheme investments perform.

Such a scheme does not cause any accounting complications in that the company's profit and loss account is the amount paid into the scheme.

Management accounts

We will conclude our consideration of profit and loss accounts by illustrating one possible format for management accounts, in summary form.

Table 5.1 sets out management accounts for a particular month's trading.

Table 5.1 *Management accounts*

	Month actual		Budgeted		Variance		Same month last year	
	£	%	£	%	£	£	£	%
Sales	281,163	100	275,000	100	6,163	252,173		100
Cost of sales	102,463	36	102,000	37	463	95,760		38
Gross profit	178,700	64	173,000	63	5,700	156,413		62
Other variable costs	67,612	24	69,000	25	(1,388)	63,446		25
Contribution	111,088	40	104,000	38	7,088	92,967		37
Fixed costs	83,170	30	80,000	29	(3,170)	75,020		30
Trading profit before interest costs	27,918	10	24,000	9	3,918	17,947		7
Interest costs	2,000	1	2,000	1	–	1,000		–
Net profit before tax	25,918	9	22,000	8	3,918	16,947		7

In this particular example, management would see the month's actual and budgeted figures. The same figures are also expressed as percentages of sales. Variances between actual and budgeted figures, both in real terms and percentage terms, are highlighted. Finally, the figures for the same month last year are shown as an additional comparative.

These summarised figures would be supported by detailed schedules with similar headings showing the breakdown of each line in detail. Key ratios would also be included. Very often, the manager in charge would append a short narrative offering explanations for variances and stating what corrective action had been taken in respect of any adverse variances.

Similar figures would be prepared on a cumulative basis for the year to date (often abbreviated to YTD).

There is an infinite variety of ways in which profit and loss accounts could be presented for management accounts purposes. The particular format chosen should be one which suits the needs of the company's management.

CHAPTER 6

Balance Sheets –
An Overview

A balance sheet is a statement of the financial position of a business at a given point in time – a snapshot of the position at the close of business on the last day in the financial year. A balance sheet is divided into two sections. The first section shows its *net asset*; the second section its *capital and reserves.*

Net assets

Assets are the resources which a business owns and which have a monetary cost. *Net assets* are those resources less all creditors and other liabilities. *Creditors* and *liabilities* are the sums which a business owes to third parties.

Those, at least, are the commonsense definitions of assets and liabilities. They hold true in over 99 per cent of cases.

Nevertheless, a recent accounting standard has redefined assets and liabilities in a more technical – and jargon-filled – way. In some very exceptional cases companies are now required to include in their balance sheets assets and liabilities which are not legally theirs.

It is not quite as bad as it at first sounds. Sometimes transactions are structured in an artificial (and invariably highly complex) manner with the deliberate aim of excluding them from a company's balance sheet. The accounting standard means the substance of such transactions now has to be taken up in the accounts. So, really, it is good news. Whenever such a situation arises, the notes to the accounts will fully disclose all the relevant facts.

There are three main constituent parts to net assets.

- *Fixed assets* are assets intended for continuing use in a company's business over a number of years.

- *Current assets* comprise cash and other assets which are not going to be held on a permanent basis.
- *Liabilities*, which are divided between liabilities falling due for payment within a year (often known as *current liabilities*) and those falling due at a later date.

Capital and reserves

The second section of the balance sheet shows how net assets have been funded.

Other general points

Like published profit and loss accounts, published balance sheets are set out in a standard format. There are two standard formats, format 1 and format 2, but format 2 is merely a horizontal version of format 1 and is rarely used.

If a company has prepared accounts under the *historical cost convention,* the value at which the assets are recorded in the balance sheet is based on what they originally cost, not their current replacement cost or selling price. The balance sheet values simply represent costs which have not yet been matched against income. Some assets, as we shall see, are recorded in the balance sheet at a valuation, but this is the exception that shows the rule. A balance sheet does not therefore represent the break-up value of a business.

The Infallible group's consolidated balance sheet is set out in Table 6.1.

Notes to the balance sheet

Published balance sheets will show the bare bones of the financial position. More detail will be shown in the notes to the accounts and each line of the balance sheet will be cross referenced to its appropriate note. The balance sheet will be contained on a single page; the notes will extend to many pages. Sometimes, many of the most important points are hidden away in the notes.

When reading a balance sheet, look first at the overall picture.

Then look at each line of the balance sheet in turn. Compare it with the figure for the previous year. Look at the note to which it is referenced to see what additional detail is given.

Balance sheets of internal accounts can be produced in any format, although in practice their layout will often closely follow that of published balance sheets.

The next four chapters look in detail at fixed assets, current assets, liabilities, and capital and reserves.

Table 6.1 *Infallible Limited consolidated balance sheet as at 31 December 1994*

	Notes	1994 £000	1994 £000	1993 £000	1993 £000
FIXED ASSETS					
Intangible assets	9	203		14	
Tangible assets	10	1,508		862	
			1,711		876
CURRENT ASSETS					
Stocks	12	2,970		2,907	
Debtors	13	3,707		2,760	
Investments	14	26		22	
Cash at bank and in hand		3		30	
		6,706		5,719	
CREDITORS – Amounts falling due within one year	15	3,602		3,258	
NET CURRENT ASSETS			3,104		2,461
TOTAL ASSETS LESS CURRENT LIABILITIES			4,815		3,337
CREDITORS – Amounts falling due after more than one year	16	707		720	
PROVISIONS FOR LIABILITIES AND CHARGES	17	21		70	
			728		790
			4,087		2,547
CAPITAL AND RESERVES					
Called up share capital	18		50		50
Share premium account			22		22
Revaluation reserve			552		–
Profit and loss account			3,436		2,453
Equity shareholders' funds			4,060		2,525
Minority interests			27		22
			4,087		2,547

CHAPTER 7

Balance Sheets – Fixed Assets

Fixed assets are those assets intended for continuing use in a company's business over a number of years which are held for the purpose of generating revenue, not for resale. When an item is included in the balance sheet as a fixed asset, it is said to be *capitalised*. Fixed assets are classified as either *intangible fixed assets* or *tangible fixed assets*.

Intangible assets are those which do not have a physical existence. Patents, licences, trade marks, goodwill, brand names and development costs are all examples of intangible assets.

Tangible assets are physical entities such as land and buildings, plant and machinery, office equipment, computers, fixtures and fittings and motor vehicles.

Let us look first at the values at which fixed assets are included in a balance sheet.

Fixed asset valuation

Fixed assets can be included in the balance sheet either at cost or at valuation. Most fixed assets are recorded at cost. The main exception is land and buildings, which is quite often shown at a valuation. In such cases, the year of the valuation will be shown, together with a note of the original cost and of the depreciation (see below) that would have been charged to date had the asset not been revalued. If the valuation was carried out in the current accounting period, the basis on which it was made and the names of the valuers will also be stated.

Most property valuations are carried out on an *open market existing use* basis. This means the value that someone would pay for it who did not intend to change fundamentally the use to which the property was put. If there is a substantial difference between the market value and book value of land and buildings, the directors are required to refer to this in the directors' report (see Chapter 13).

Some categories of land and buildings, known as *investment properties*, are always included in the accounts at their open market value, due to the requirements of accounting standards. An investment property is a property which is held for its investment value and is not used in the business.

Depreciation

Nothing lasts for ever and fixed assets are no exception. As a consequence, the book values of all fixed assets (other than investment properties) are charged systematically to profit and loss account over the assets' expected useful lives. The charge concerned is called *depreciation*. Depreciation represents that part of the cost or previous value which has been used up in operating the business. It is calculated by estimating how long an asset will last, and what it will be worth at the end of its useful life.

This calculation is often based on guesswork. Who knows how long a machine will last or what it will be worth, if anything, at the end of its life? Accordingly, accounts are required to show the amount of depreciation charged to the profit and loss account and the basis on which it has been calculated. Some companies show the depreciation rates used (eg 10 or 20 per cent per annum) and some show the estimated useful lives (eg 10 or 5 years). It comes to the same thing, provided that the depreciation rate used is applied on a straight line basis.

The *straight line basis* of calculating depreciation simply means that the depreciation rate is applied to the original cost (or valuation) of the asset each year, as in all the examples used in this book. An alternative method is the *reducing balance basis*. Under this method the depreciation rate is applied to what is left of the cost (or valuation) after deducting depreciation charged in previous years.

The Infallible group uses the straight line basis and discloses the rates used in its list of accounting policies, specifically in Note 1(d).

You should look closely at asset lives disclosed in the accounts to see whether they make sense. If they have been underestimated, depreciation charged to the profit and loss account will be higher than it should be and reported profits will be lower. Correspondingly, the book value of assets in the balance sheet will be on the low side.

Where fixed assets have been revalued upwards, depreciation will be based on that valuation rather than the original cost. Accordingly, depreciation will be higher than it would have been had it been based on original cost; the profit for the year will be correspondingly lower.

For internal decision-making purposes, many users are more interested in finding out what it would cost to replace an asset when its useful life is over than in how much of its previous cost or valuation has been used up. Assets might therefore be included in management accounts at the sum it would cost to replace them, with depreciation based on that figure. Depreciation would then represent how much should be set aside to replace the asset when it eventually wears out.

Intangible assets

Intangible assets are required by law to be classified in published balance sheets between:

- Development costs
- Concessions, licences, patents, trade marks and similar rights and assets
- Goodwill
- Payments on account.

Most of these headings are self-explanatory, but the headings development costs and goodwill require some comment.

Development costs

Development costs are those costs incurred in *using* scientific or technical knowledge to produce new or substantially improved products or services. Accountants distinguish them from *pure and applied research costs*, which are costs incurred in *obtaining* new scientific or technical knowledge, either for its own sake (pure research) or directed towards a practical aim (applied research).

Accounting standards require both pure and applied costs to be charged to the profit and loss account in the year in which they are incurred. However, development costs can be included as an intangible asset in the balance sheet if they meet *all* the following criteria:

- There is a clearly defined project on which the related expenditure is separately identifiable.
- The technical feasibility and ultimate commercial viability of the project has been assessed with reasonable certainty.
- The end product is likely to be profitable.
- The project is likely to be completed!

As with other fixed assets, capitalised development costs which are included in the balance sheet have to be depreciated – but only after the end product has been brought into commercial production.

The accounting policy adopted for development costs will be set out in the list of accounting policies. Our advice is to be pretty wary of any costs capitalised as development costs.

Public companies (and large private companies) will disclose the amount of research and development expenditure charged to the profit and loss account in the year.

Goodwill

When a company buys another profitable business, it will often pay more for it than the market value, or fair value, of its individual net assets. Such a premium is called *goodwill* by accountants. The term can be misleading to the non-accountant who may think that it means more than it actually does. *All* it represents is the premium over the current market value of the individual assets paid by a particular buyer at a particular point in time.

Accountants believe that a premium will only be paid if a business is generating more profits than could reasonably be expected from its asset value which they see as a situation which cannot last indefinitely. Therefore, they insist that goodwill has to be written off, either straight away or over a period.

Few non-accountants agree with this view. It is an area of continuing controversy.

Strangely enough, if a group writes off goodwill straight away (as the Infallible group does), its profits *for the year* will *not* be affected. This is because FRS 3 requires it to be written off in a way which does not affect the profit for the year (see Chapter 12). On the other hand, if the group writes off goodwill over a period of years, the charge each year will be treated as a normal charge against profits.

The situation is a mess. The accounts of groups which write off goodwill straight away are really not comparable with those which write it off over a period of time. Extreme caution should be applied when making comparisons between companies adopting different policies. The accounting policy adopted by any group will be set out in its list of accounting policies.

One other point on goodwill: accounting standards permit goodwill to be recorded in a balance sheet only when a premium has actually been paid to a third party.

Acquisition accounting and merger accounting

Underlying what we have written so far about goodwill has been the assumption that, when one company buys another, it accounts for it by a method of accounting known as *acquisition accounting*.

Acquisition accounting is a method which is used when one company buys ('acquires') another. The two distinctive features of acquisition accounting are, firstly, that a figure for goodwill is thrown up in the acquiring company's consolidated balance sheet if it pays more for its new subsidiary than the fair value of that subsidiary's assets: and, secondly, that the profits of the acquired company are only included in the group's profit and loss account for the period after acquisition.

However, when two companies merge, instead of one company taking over the other, an alternative method called *merger accounting* can be used.

Under merger accounting no figure for goodwill will arise in the group balance sheet. All the problems associated with accounting for goodwill thereby disappear. A further advantage is that the group profit and loss account will include the profits of both companies for the period *before* the date of acquisition as well as the period after.

Because merger accounting usually makes the figures look better, acquisitions have in the past frequently been structured in such a way that, technically, they counted as mergers, in order that merger accounting could be used. This particular loop hole has now been closed by a new accounting standard, but only for accounting periods starting on or after 23 December 1994.

Brand names

Closely associated with the controversy surrounding goodwill is one about brand names.

Sometimes a company will buy a business whose products have well-known brand names which are not reflected in its balance sheet. Traditionally, the premium paid for such brand names would have been included in the figure for goodwill. Recently, some companies have allocated part of the cost of such acquisitions to brand names and then recorded the brand names separately in their group balance sheet. The figure for goodwill is thereby reduced since part of it is shown as 'brand names'.

Groups which follow this practice then go one stage further. They refuse to depreciate the figure for brand names on the grounds that they spend a great deal of money on advertising and promoting them in order to keep their value intact. Since such groups would have been forced to write off or depreciate the appropriate sum if it had been included in goodwill, they thereby boost their profits.

Other companies have gone further still. They have capitalised brand names which they have built up themselves rather than purchased from a third party. By doing this, they have effectively circumvented the rule that a company can include goodwill in its balance sheet only for premiums actually paid to third parties. Some companies have included brand names at *current cost*, meaning the amount which they would have to spend today to buy them.

One or two companies have been more sophisticated. They

have capitalised brand names at figures which they say represent the incremental earnings expected to arise from the ownership of the brands. What they mean is the extra profits they can make by putting a brand name on a product as compared with selling the same product unbranded. Specialised consultancies calculate the appropriate figure for them.

At least one group has even included a figure for certain of its companies' names in its balance sheet, described rather grandly as 'corporate brand names'!

What are we to make of all this? For our own part we go back to our watchwords: scepticism and caution. We would adopt a sceptical attitude to such practices. We would be cautious about those groups which follow them. (Such caution might not be misplaced. Some of the companies which have adopted the most 'innovative' practices subsequently found themselves in the most financial difficulties.)

Above all, we would ask for consistency between companies. Only some groups owning brand names capitalise them. Many others with equally valuable brands do not. When you look at groups with brand names in their balance sheets, you should make a mental adjustment both to the total of the balance sheet and to reported profits.

Intangible assets in the Infallible group's consolidated balance sheet are analysed in Note 9 to the accounts.

Tangible assets

Tangible fixed assets are analysed, usually in a note, under headings appropriate to the business.

The following categories are set out in the Companies Act:

- Land and buildings
- Plant and machinery
- Fixtures, fittings, tools and equipment
- Payments on account and assets in course of construction.

These categories are fairly self-explanatory. The figures for land and buildings, which are always shown separately from other fixed assets, are split between properties which are freehold, long lease-hold (leases with more than 50 years unexpired) and short lease-hold. Investment properties are also always separately identified.

You will therefore get quite a reasonable picture of the types of property owned by a company.

A note to the accounts will always show additions and disposals in the year, together with details of depreciation, for all fixed assets, together with details of depreciation. A shrewd reader of the accounts will also look at the cash flow statement (see Chapter 11) to find the sale proceeds of disposals.

The Infallible group's note on tangible fixed assets (Note 10 to the accounts) is reproduced in Table 7.1.

Table 7.1 *Note on tangible fixed assets*

	Freehold land and buildings £000	Plant and machinery £000	Fixtures and equipment £000	Motor vehicles £000	Total £000
Group and company					
Cost or valuation					
At 1 January 1994	717	208	50	33	1,008
Additions	–	112	48	83	243
Surplus on revaluation	483	–	–	–	483
Disposals	–	(27)	–	(34)	(61)
At 31 December 1994	1,200	293	98	82	1,673
Depreciation					
At 1 January 1994	56	64	18	8	146
Charge for the year	13	61	13	27	114
Surplus on revaluation	(69)	–	–	–	(69)
Disposals	–	(18)	–	(8)	(26)
At 31 December 1994	–	107	31	27	165
Net book value					
At 31 December 1994	1,200	186	67	55	1,508
At 31 December 1993	661	144	32	25	862

The freehold land and buildings, which had previously been accounted for under the historical cost rules, were revalued on 31 December 1994 on an open market value basis by Gessit & Partners, chartered surveyors.

The historical cost and related depreciation of the freehold land and buildings is set out below:

	£000
Historical cost at 31 December 1994	717
Accumulated historical depreciation	(69)
Historical cost net book value at 31 December 1994	648

All other tangible fixed assets are stated under the historical rules. The net book value of plant and machinery includes an amount of £180,000 (1993:£136,000) in respect of assets held under finance leases and hire-purchase contracts.

The note gives the details referred to earlier in the chapter concerning the freehold land and buildings included at a valuation.

The note also gives details about assets held under *hire-purchase* contracts and *finance leases*. These are included in fixed assets even though, strictly speaking, they are not legally owned by the business.

Under a *finance lease*, the person who leases the asset (the lessee) enjoys almost all the rewards of ownership and takes on almost all the risks. The lessee is able to use the asset over virtually all its useful life; it will hardly ever be leased to anyone else once the lease has expired. Assets leased under such arrangements must be capitalised in the balance sheet as fixed assets and the future leasing payment obligations are taken into the balance sheet as liabilities.

Fixed asset investments

There is a further class of fixed assets not previously mentioned, called *fixed asset investments*. These are investments treated by the directors as long-term holdings.

Fixed asset investments will be analysed in a note to the accounts between investments in subsidiary undertakings, associated undertakings and other investments. Other investments in turn will be split between listed and unlisted investments. If any investments suffer a permanent fall in value, they will normally be written down.

Investments in subsidiary undertakings will appear only in the parent company's balance sheet and not that of the group, with further particulars of the companies concerned being set out in a note.

Table 7.2 (overleaf) sets out an extract from the notes to Infallible's accounts which gives details of the subsidiaries.

Future capital expenditure

A separate note usually found towards the end of the accounts (Note 19 for the Infallible group), will show how much future capital expenditure has been authorised by the directors but not yet contracted. It will also show the value of any contracts made where the assets have not been acquired by the balance sheet date. This will at least give some indication of a company's future capital expenditure programme.

Table 7.2 *Details of subsidiaries*

Investments	1994 £000	1993 £000
Shares in group undertakings – at cost	219	219

| Name of company and country of incorporation | Description of shares held | Proportion held | | Activity |
		Direct	Indirect	
Bertie Limited (England)	Ordinary shares	100%	–	Manufacture of colour designs
Cecil Limited (Scotland)	Ordinary shares	100%	–	Designers
Dellboy Limited (England)	Ordinary shares	–	75%	Designers of colour designs

CHAPTER 8

Balance Sheets –
Current Assets

Current assets comprise cash and other assets which are going to
be converted into cash and are not going to be held by a business
on a permanent basis.
The current assets of the Infallible group are set out in Table
8.1.

Table 8.1 *Current assets*

	1994 £000	1993 £000
Stocks	2,970	2,907
Debtors	3,707	2,760
Investments	26	22
Cash at bank and in hand	3	30
	6,706	5,719

Stocks

Stocks are classified in published accounts under three headings.
The Infallible group's stocks are set out under these three headings in Note 12 to its accounts, an extract from which is reproduced in Table 8.2.
   Payments on account received against any items would be
shown separately as a deduction. This is particularly important
for contractors, such as builders.

Raw materials and consumables
For manufacturers, raw materials comprise items bought for use
in the manufacturing process but on which no manufacturing

operation has yet been carried out. Generally, retail and service companies do not buy raw materials.

Table 8.2 *Stocks*

	1994 £000	1993 £000
Raw materials and consumables	629	656
Work in progress	1,205	981
Finished goods and goods for resale	1,136	1,270
	2,970	2,907

Consumables comprise items which are used by a business in the course of its operations but are not sold by it and which do not form part of the product which it sells. Consumables might include items such as stationery or cleaning materials. Since these have nothing to do with the output of a business they are different in kind from other types of stock. Such items are usually insignificant in total and are often not counted. Raw materials and consumables are bracketed together for disclosure purposes in published accounts.

Work in progress

For manufacturers, work in progress comprises goods on which the manufacturing process has been started, but not yet completed. The goods could be at any stage of production. Retailers and wholesalers do not have any work in progress since they do not carry out any processing of the goods which they hold. Companies which sell services could have work in progress, which in their case would consist of costs incurred up to the balance sheet date in commencing work on a service which had not been completed.

Finished goods and goods for resale

For manufacturers, finished goods and goods for resale are goods manufactured for resale but not yet sold.

Sometimes such goods will have been sent on consignment to customers who themselves intend to sell them on to another customer. For instance, motor car manufacturers send cars to dealers who attempt to sell them to the general public. In legal terms, ownership is usually retained by the manufacturer. In the past, such goods would usually be included as stock in the manufacturer's balance sheet and excluded from the dealer's balance sheet. Under the new accounting standard *Reporting the Substance of Transactions*, however, there may be circumstances under which such stock is included in the dealer's balance sheet and excluded from the manufacturer's. It will all depend on who really bears the risk and who has the benefits which are associated with the stock. Deciding upon that – deciding upon the substance of the transaction – will be a matter of judgment on which different accountants may take differing views.

For retailers or wholesalers, finished goods comprise goods purchased for resale but not yet sold. Service companies have no stock of finished goods, since they do not sell goods.

Stock valuation

Stocks are included in published accounts at the lower of cost and net realisable value. They are not valued at their selling price. This is a very important valuation principle which it is vital to understand fully.

This valuation basis follows on logically from two fundamental accounting principles. The first is the matching principle, which we have already encountered. This states that expenditure should always be matched to the revenue which it generates. Stocks of raw materials represent costs which have been incurred but which have not yet generated revenue, because the goods are still in their raw state. Work in progress represents costs incurred which have not generated revenue because the end result is not yet in a fit state to be sold. Stocks of finished goods and goods for resale represents costs incurred on goods which are ready to be sold, but where no sale has been made. Stocks of consumables represent costs incurred on items which have not been used in the current accounting period.

While the matching principle states that costs and revenues

ought to be matched, the prudence principle states that revenue should not be anticipated before it has been earned. Therefore all that can be done is to carry forward unmatched costs to the next accounting period when they can be matched to revenues which it is hoped they will generate.

Therefore, all that the figure for stocks included in the balance sheet represents is the carrying forward of costs from one accounting period to the next only. That is why stocks should never be valued at anything higher than cost – to do so would be to anticipate a profit which has not yet been, and may not be, earned.

Costs

The costs at which stocks are valued should represent the prices actually paid for the items in question, not the prices prevailing at the balance sheet date, which may well be higher.

Example

A business with a financial year end of 31 December buys 200 boxes of raw materials in July at a cost of £100 per box and still holds 50 boxes at 31 December. Their stock value is £5,000 (50 × £100). This is still true even though the suppliers put the price up to £105 per box in September.

The business also buys 100 further boxes of the same items in October at £105 per box, and still holds 10 of these boxes at 31 December. These are valued at £1,050 (10 × £105).

The total stock valuation is £6,050. Two acquisitions of exactly the same raw materials are valued at two different prices, because they cost two different prices.

That is a simple example involving two deliveries and one price rise.

Many businesses have hundreds of lines of stock. Each line may go up in price two or three times in the year. The price rises on different lines of stock may occur at different times.

How do we know that, if we have 60 items in stock, they represent 50 deliveries in July and 10 deliveries in October, and not some other combination? Bear in mind that stock records are often much less well kept than other accounting records.

Various conventions are used. Some of the more common are set out below, together with the effect which they would have on stock valuation in our example.

FIFO

FIFO (first in, first out) values stock on the basis that stock delivered first is used first. On this basis, the 60 boxes of stock in hand at the end of December would all be valued at September prices since it would be assumed that the July deliveries had all been utilised. The result would be a stock valuation of £6,300 (60 ×£105), which would be £250 higher than the true value of £6,050.

Average price

Average price takes the average price for each line of stock during the stockholding period. The stocks in our example would be valued at an average price of £102.50 (£100 + £105, divided by 2). This gives a stock valuation of £6,150 (60 × £102.50), which is £100 higher than the true value of £6,050.

Weighted average price

Weighted average price takes the weighted average price for each line of stock during the stockholding period, calculated as follows:

	£
200 × £100	20,000
100 × £105	10,500
300	30,500

The weighted average is £101.67 (£30,500 divided by 300).

This gives a stock value of £6,100 (60 × £101.67), which is £50 higher than the true valuation of £6,050.

LIFO

LIFO (last in, first out) is a very conservative method which values stock on the basis of the earliest line still held. It would value stock at £6,000 (60 × £100). This method is unacceptable in the UK for accounts required to show a true and fair view, but is widely used in the USA.

Replacement price

A method sometimes used for management accounting purposes (but which is unacceptable for true and fair view accounts) is replacement price. This values stock at what it would cost to replace at the relevant date. For the decision-making process it can be a very useful measure of value. It would value the stock in our example at £6,300 (60 × £105), assuming no further price rises after September. If there had been a further price rise in December of £2 to £107 then it would use this price and value the stock at £6,420 (60 × £107).

If there is a significant difference between the value of stocks in the balance sheet and their replacement price, the difference will be shown in a note to the accounts.

Manufacturing companies

There are additional inherent difficulties for manufacturing businesses in valuing work in progress and finished goods. The values must include all production costs. How should production costs be allocated to individual lines? Which overheads should be included and what should the basis be? Service companies can have similar problems in valuing work in progress.

Taken together, all the difficulties of valuing stock mean that an element of uncertainty *always* surrounds the final figure. This is so even when everyone starts off with the best intentions. In those cases where management's intentions are not quite as pure as the driven snow, they have scope, within broad limits, to manipulate the final stock figure. Estimate piles upon estimate, approximation upon approximation, and the final figure wobbles uncertainly upon those often less than solid foundations. And every £1 increase in the value of stock at the end of the year means an extra £1 of reported profit.

Net realisable value

The prudence principle, in addition to saying that revenues and profits should not be anticipated, also states that provision should be made for losses as soon as they can be foreseen. In some instances, lines of stock and work in progress will have a net realisable value which is lower than cost. The *net realisable value* of stock is the price at which it could be sold in the ordinary course of business in the condition in which it existed at the balance sheet date, less any costs which would be incurred in selling it.

We stress the words 'in the ordinary course of business'. Net realisable value on a forced sale would probably be lower. However, the going concern principle means that accounts are prepared on the basis that a business will continue in operation.

The net realisable value of stock may be less than its cost because it has been damaged, or rendered obsolete, or because of a lack of demand, or simply because the market is saturated and the selling price has fallen.

In all cases where the net realisable value has fallen below cost, the prudence principle dictates that the loss which will clearly arise when the stock comes to be sold should be anticipated and provided for in the accounts straight away. In such cases, stock should be written down below cost to its net realisable value.

Sometimes, businesses will write down stock below its cost price where none of the factors set out above specifically apply, but where the lines of stock in question are very slow moving. This may be justified on the grounds that, because the stock is slow moving, an element of uncertainty exists as to its eventual sale, and/or further costs will be incurred in holding it prior to its eventual sale.

The accounting policy adopted by the Infallible group is as follows:

> 'Stocks are stated at the lower of cost and net realisable value. Cost is determined on a first-in, first-out basis. The cost of work in progress and finished goods comprises materials, direct labour and attributable production overheads. Net realisable value is based on estimated selling price less any further costs which are expected to be incurred to completion and disposal.'

This is a common form of accounting policy.

Long-term contracts
Work in progress may include long-term contracts. A *long-term*

contract is a significant contract where the length of the contract straddles more than one accounting period. Such a contract will usually, but not necessarily, last more than one year.

Such contracts abound in the construction industry. Suppose a company worked on a major contract which lasted five years, and this was the only contract it had. Peculiar results would occur if normal stock rules were followed. Suppose the costs incurred on such a contract amounted to £10 million, spread over five years, and the final profit on the contract was £5 million at the end of the fifth year. In the first four years of the contract the company would not show any profits at all. In the fifth year a profit of £5 million would suddenly appear. But would it all have been earned then, or would some of it be attributed to work done over the previous four years?

Accountants think the latter and have developed an accounting standard which effectively says that the profit which arises at the end of the contract should be anticipated and spread over the entire period of the contract. (Any loss should be recognised straight away and in full.)

Likewise, the company's turnover will reflect the value of work done on the contract to date. The accounting entries are complex, even if the principle is simple, and they will sometimes throw up a figure in debtors called *amounts recoverable on contracts*, which represents the difference between the figure recorded as turnover and payments requested on account to date. It is quite normal.

Stock to turnover ratio

One of the most popular operating ratios is to compare stocks with turnover and then express the result in months. The calculation is as follows:

$$\frac{\text{Stock}}{\text{Turnover}} \times 12$$

Example
The Infallible group's stocks at the year end are £2,970,000 and turnover on continuing operations (including acquisitions) is

£17,911,000. Stocks represent two months' turnover, calculated thus:

$$\frac{2,970,000}{17,911,000} \times 12 = 2\,\text{months}$$

The comparable figure for 1993 (based on continuing operations) was 2.4 months, which shows that the group has become more efficient in holding stock.

Of course, this is not exactly comparing like with like since turnover includes a profit element whereas stocks, except in the case of long-term contracts, do not.

Stockholding period

A better method is to compare stocks with cost of sales, which can be done in those instances where companies publish format 1 profit and loss accounts.

Example
According to Note 3 to the accounts, the Infallible group's cost of sales on continuing operations (including acquisitions) is £6,152,000. The stockholding period is 5.8 months:

$$\frac{2,970,000}{6,152,000} \times 12 = 5.8\,\text{months}$$

This is rather a different story! The comparable figure for 1993 (based on continuing operations) was 6.6 months.

As with all ratios, the results are of most value when used to make comparisons with competitors and with previous years.

Most companies try to keep a balance between holding the minimum amount of stock necessary to run their business, thereby minimising the amount of working capital which they require (with just-in-time stockholding policies becoming increasingly common) and holding enough stock to avoid suffering unforeseen shortages, with a corresponding loss of sales. Again, as with all such performance ratios, it is up to the user of the accounts to decide what he thinks is a good figure for this ratio. There are no absolute rights or wrongs.

Management accounts ought to identify occasions when stock levels of key items are in danger of falling below the minimum level necessary for the business to operate efficiently. If stock is held at more than one location it may be necessary to identify the different locations.

Readers of management accounts should also be clear as to the reliability (or otherwise!) of the underlying stock records and valuation bases on which the figures in those accounts are based.

Debtors

Debtors are sums of money owed to a business. Debtors are sometimes known as *monetary assets*, which means that they are assets which will be turned into money. Debtors shown in the balance sheet will be analysed in a note to published accounts between amounts falling due within one year of the balance sheet date and any amounts falling due later. Both categories will then be sub-analysed.

The Infallible group does not have any debtors falling due more than one year from the balance sheet date. Its debtors falling due within one year are analysed in Note 13 to the accounts, which is reproduced in Table 8.3.

Table 8.3 *Debtors – amounts falling due within one year*

	1994		1993	
	Group	Company	Group	Company
	£000	£000	£000	£000
Trade debtors	3,243	2,699	2,382	2,025
Amounts owed by subsidiary undertakings	–	96	–	70
Advance corporation tax recoverable	–	–	8	8
Other debtors	173	173	140	140
Prepayments and accrued income	291	275	230	219
	3,707	3,243	2,760	2,462

Let us look at the largest item first.

Trade debtors
Trade debtors are invoiced sales which have not yet been paid by the customer. They include VAT. If any debts are considered to

be bad or doubtful, a provision will be made against them and deducted from trade debtors. Such a provision will be separately identified in management accounts. Any provisions made for the issue of future credit notes against past sales will also be deducted.

Debt-collection period
Trade debtors can be expressed as a percentage of turnover which, in turn, can be expressed as a debt-collection period in terms of months. The calculation is as follows:

$$\frac{\text{Trade debtors}}{\text{Turnover}} \times 12$$

Example
The Infallible group's turnover on continuing operations (including acquisitions) is £17,911,000 and its trade debtors at the balance sheet date are £3,243,000. Its debt-collection period at that date is 2.2 months, calculated thus:

$$\frac{3,243,000}{17,911,000} \times 12 = 2.2 \text{ months}$$

The comparable figure for 1993 (based on continuing operations) was 2.0 months, which shows that the collection of debtors has deteriorated.

The lower the debt-collection period, the better for the company. This is one instance where absolute rules do apply!

Although this is a most useful ratio, it must still be treated with some caution. The company's business may be seasonal. If it happens to make only 20 per cent of its sales in the last three months of the year, its apparent debt-collection period will be lower than it really is. For management accounting purposes, it is much better to calculate the debt-collection period by considering sales over the period immediately leading up to the balance sheet date. The calculation is illustrated overleaf:

Example

		£000	
Sales:	January – August	14,329	
	September	963	
	October	1,046	
	November	587	
	December	986	
		17,911	

		£000	Months
Debtors at 31 December		3,243	
Less:	December sales	986	1.0
		2,257	
Less:	November sales	587	1.0
		1,670	
Less:	October sales	1,046	1.0
Balance		624	
Balance as proportion of September sales		624 ÷ 963	= 0.6
			3.6

Debtors at 31 December therefore represent 3.6 months' sales, which is rather different from 2.2 months. Even so, it is still only a guide. It might be that trade debtors of £3,243,000 included some old July debts still outstanding. The figure of 3.6 months is only an average.

Turnover in published accounts excludes VAT whereas trade debtors generally include VAT. This is the same for all businesses in the UK, and it therefore has no great significance when comparisons of UK companies are made. If turnover, however, includes a significant element of cash sales or exports, this will distort the ratio since only credit sales give rise to trade debtors and no VAT is charged on exports.

Factoring debtors

Some companies boost their cash resources by *factoring* their debtors. This is where a company sells the debts from its customers to a factoring company for immediate cash. On a *without-recourse* basis, the factoring company suffers the loss if a customer does not pay. On a *with-recourse* basis, the factoring company claims the money back from the supplier company if the customer does not pay. The supplier company suffers the loss.

The usual practice when debts were factored used to be to deduct cash received from the factoring company from the amount of debtors shown in the balance sheet. If factoring was without recourse, the amount concerned would be indicated in the note on contingent liabilities (see Chapter 9). Apart from this note, which could easily be missed, there would be no indication that a company had factored its debtors.

A new accounting standard, effective for periods ended on or after 22 September 1994, has changed all that.

If debts are factored without recourse then two accounting treatments are now possible. If it simply sells the debts to the factoring company for a single, non-returnable fixed sum then the old treatment (now graced with a name – *derecognition*) can be followed.

If, however, it receives only some of the cash immediately with the balance dependent upon whether the debtor pays, or it pays interest on the amount paid by the factoring company until it in turn is paid by the debtor, then in one way or another the benefits it receives are still linked to the performance of the debt. In such a case it may follow what is called a *linked presentation*. Under this, the non-returnable proceeds will be deducted from debtors on the face of the balance sheet as follows:

	£
Debts factored without recourse:	
Debtors	970,000
Less: non-returnable proceeds	800,000
	170,000

A company in that position will give full details in a note to the accounts.

If debts are factored with recourse then the debts will stay on the balance sheet, with the amount advanced by the factoring company being shown as a loan under current liabilities. This is known as *separate presentation*.

We shall now move on to the other elements of debtors, which are usually much less significant than trade debtors.

Amounts owed by subsidiary undertakings

Any amounts owed to the reporting company by group companies will be shown separately. Amounts owed to the reporting company by associated undertakings are also shown separately.

Advance corporation tax recoverable

Infallible's accounts show advance corporation tax recoverable in 1993 which represented ACT (see Chapter 3) due on the proposed final dividend for that year. This would have been recovered in 1994 by way of offset against Infallible's mainstream corporation tax liability.

The ACT recoverable on the proposed final dividend for 1994 has been accounted for by being deducted from Infallible's deferred tax liability (see Chapter 9). In 1993, Infallible had no deferred tax liability.

Prepayments and accrued income

Prepayments are expenses paid during the current period which relate to a future period. Most prepayments are time-related expenses paid in advance such as rent and insurance.

If prepayments are significant in size, they should be examined carefully to see that all items genuinely relate to future periods and not to the current period. It is a well-known practice for managers to try to carry forward expenditure so as to increase their profits for the current year.

Prepayments could include pension cost prepayments, where payments made are greater than the expected long-term regular pension cost (see Chapter 5).

Accrued income is any income which has been earned by the company but has not yet been invoiced by it. It is comparatively rare.

Other debtors

Other debtors will include any debtors which do not fit into any of the other categories. Some companies obtain VAT refunds and any such refunds due at the balance sheet date would be included under this category. A few companies make loans to their directors (which is illegal for amounts over £5,000). Such loans must be separately disclosed. Very often they are included under the category of other debtors with a supplementary note stating that other debtors include loans to directors and giving the relevant details.

Foreign currency

Any debtors denominated in a foreign currency are usually retranslated into sterling at the rate of exchange ruling at the end of the financial year, unless a special rate has been fixed. Reference should be made to the list of accounting policies to see the basis of translation. The accounting policy of the Infallible group is as follows:

> 'Transactions in foreign currencies are recorded at the rate ruling at the date of the transaction. Monetary assets and liabilities denominated in foreign currency are retranslated at the rate of exchange ruling at the balance sheet date. All exchange differences are taken to the profit and loss account.'

(The reference to 'differences' is because foreign currency items would originally have been translated into sterling at the rate ruling at the invoice date.)

It is certainly worth showing debtors designated in foreign currency separately in management accounts, as a way of highlighting and monitoring the uncertainties associated with them. The rate of exchange used should also be shown. In addition to the difficulties in actually collecting amounts owed by overseas debtors, movements in currency rates can mean that the eventual sterling equivalent of the amount collected is significantly different from the sums originally intended.

Investments

Investments which are not held on a long-term basis, or for use in the business, are included as current assets in the balance sheet. If they are quoted investments their market value will be noted in published accounts in addition to their cost. That is the case with the Infallible group.

Cash at bank and in hand

By convention, the figure shown in the accounts will be the figure shown in the company's cash book, not the figure shown by the bank statement. Banks do not always agree with this presentation, particularly if it results in an unauthorised bank overdraft appearing in the accounts. The two figures will be reconciled by the company accountant, the reconciling items being cheques entered in the cash book but not yet presented to the bank, and money paid into the bank and entered in the cash book which has not yet appeared on the bank statement.

As with debtors, any bank balances designated in a foreign currency will be translated into sterling, usually at the rate of exchange ruling at the balance sheet date.

CHAPTER 9

Balance Sheets – Liabilities

Liabilities (which may alternatively be called *creditors*) are sums of money owed by a business to third parties. In published accounts they will be shown on two separate lines on the balance sheet as *amounts falling due within one year* and *amounts falling due after more than one year* from the balance sheet date.

Amounts falling due within one year are often referred to as *current liabilities*. Most creditors which arise in the normal course of trade will fall within this category as will ordinary bank overdrafts, which are theoretically repayable on demand.

The sums included in *amounts falling due after more than one year* will usually consist of longer-term loans from banks, hire-purchase companies, finance companies and other lenders. A note to the accounts will show how much is repayable between one and two years of the balance sheet date, between two and five years from that date and more than five years from that date. (For obligations under finance leases and hire-purchase contracts – see page 81 – the first two categories will be lumped together.) Where loans are repayable by instalments, the proportion due for payment in the next 12 months will be shown separately in current liabilities.

If any borrowings are repayable wholly or in part more than five years from the balance sheet date, details about the terms of repayment and rates of interest will be included in a note to the accounts.

If a company has given security to third parties for any amounts owed to them, by giving them a charge over particular assets – or over all assets – the details will also be given. This applies to all liabilities whether current or not.

Finally, details of any loans which are convertible into share capital will be given.

You therefore get pretty full details of a company's borrowing structure and will be able to form your own view of its financial stability. So can the company's banks and suppliers!

Creditors

The Infallible group's creditors falling due within one year are set out in Note 15, which is reproduced in Table 9.1. Amounts falling due after more than one year are shown separately in Note 16 to the group's accounts. The headings within the two notes are similar.

Table 9.1 *Creditors – Amounts falling due within one year*

	1994		1993	
	Group	Company	Group	Company
	£000	*£000*	*£000*	*£000*
Debenture loan	90	90	90	90
Bank loans and overdrafts	448	448	870	870
Obligations under finance leases and hire-purchase contracts	50	50	34	34
Trade creditors	1,942	1,895	1,581	1,554
Corporation tax	644	637	350	346
Advance corporation tax payable	22	22	8	8
Other taxation and social security	187	171	149	141
Other creditors	91	83	70	66
Accruals and deferred income	53	44	81	71
Proposed final dividend	75	75	25	25
	3,602	3,515	3,258	3,205

The bank loans and overdrafts are secured by a floating charge over the assets of the company.

Let us look at each of the headings.

Debenture loans

A debenture loan is made to a company which is secured on its assets by way of a legal charge. Such a charge may be either a *fixed* or *floating charge. Fixed charges* are fixed on specific assets of the company. *Floating charges* are not fixed on specific assets but float over assets which, by their nature, are likely to change or be substituted in the ordinary course of a company's business. Such assets might include stock or debtors, the individual items of which are always changing, even though the totals may remain fairly constant.

The proportion of the loan repayable more than 12 months after the balance sheet date is included in Note 16. Since some of it is repayable more than five years in the future, Note 16 also gives details of repayment terms and the interest rate.

Bank loans and overdrafts

This is a self-explanatory heading. In published accounts, positive bank balances have their own separate line on the balance sheet (together with cash in hand) but bank loans and overdrafts are included, together with all other amounts owed by the business, under the heading creditors. Where a company has both a positive bank balance and a bank overdraft and there is a legal right of set-off (as there usually is) only the net figure will be shown in the published balance sheet.

It is very common for a bank loan or bank overdraft to be secured on a company's assets and, as we said before, details of the security will be disclosed.

In internal accounts, bank overdrafts will invariably be shown separately from creditors, and bank loans will be shown as separate items.

Obligations under finance leases and hire-purchase contracts

These represent borrowings incurred as a result of acquiring assets under hire-purchase contracts or finance leases, previously discussed in Chapter 7.

The item 'finance charges allocated to future periods' in Note 16 simply means the interest that will be payable in the future.

Trade creditors

Trade creditors disclose the amounts owed for goods and services used by a business in the ordinary course of its trade. As such, they include the VAT element of the original invoice. In most companies, the sums included under the heading of trade creditors will be the creditors shown on the company's *creditors' ledger*. Many companies call this ledger a *purchase ledger* or *bought ledger*.

Credit payment period

It is possible to calculate the approximate period of credit taken by a company from its suppliers from the information available in the accounts. A profit and loss account produced under format 1 will show the figures for cost of sales, distribution costs and administrative expenses. Some, perhaps all, of these will include labour costs, but the figure for those costs will be available from a note to the accounts. The figure for depreciation may also be deducted. In the Infallible group's case, the figures for continuing activities (including acquisitions) are:

	1994	1993
	£000	£000
Cost of sales	6,152	5,252
Distribution costs	4,073	3,440
Administrative expenses (all shown in Note 3 to the accounts)	5,375	4,452
	15,600	13,144
Labour costs (shown in Note 23 to the accounts)	(4,540)	(4,256)
	11,060	8,888
Less: Depreciation (shown in Note 6 to the accounts)	(138)	(87)
	10,922	8,801

These can then be compared with trade creditors. The result will be an approximation since trade creditors include VAT whereas the expenses do not, but this is the same for all UK companies. It may also be the case that some relevant expense creditors will be included under the heading of 'other creditors' or 'accruals and deferred income' (see page 104), but this is unlikely to have a significant effect on the calculation in most cases.

The credit payment period is calculated as follows:

$$\frac{\text{Trade creditors}}{\text{Non-labour expenses}} \times 12$$

The result is expressed in terms of months, showing the average period of credit taken by the company.

Example

The Infallible group has trade creditors of £1,942,000. Non-labour expenses are £10,922,000. The average period of credit taken by the company is:

$$\frac{1,942,000}{10,922,000} \times 12 = 2.1 \text{ months}$$

The comparable figure for the previous year was 2.2 months.

Unusually, the group appears to be using some of the cash which it generates from its operations to pay its suppliers more quickly!

The calculation is sometimes made using the figure for cost of sales instead of the figure for non-labour expenses – but cost of sales might include manufacturing wages and salaries in the case of a manufacturing company.

If the profit and loss account is prepared under format 2, the following items can be added together and compared with trade creditors:

- Change in stocks of finished goods and work in progress
- Own work capitalised
- Raw materials and consumables
- Other external charges
- Other operating charges.

None of these items should include labour costs which are included on a separate line of their own in format 2 profit and loss accounts.

The difficulties of finding an appropriate measure of costs from format 1 profit and loss accounts with which to compare trade creditors, mean that some people compare trade creditors with the company's turnover. There is no particular logic to this but it can give useful comparative results when comparing different years. It can also be useful for comparing different companies in the same industry where those different companies have similar gross and net profits.

Other taxation and social security

The 'taxation' element of the heading includes VAT not yet paid over to Customs & Excise and PAYE not paid over to the Inland Revenue. It could also include excise duty and Advance Corporation Tax payable on proposed dividends, although the Infallible group shows ACT separately.

Corporation Tax payable is shown on a separate line and will not necessarily be the same as the tax charge in the profit and loss account. The balance sheet figure might include unpaid Corporation Tax relating to the previous year and is stated after deducting any payments made for ACT.

'Social security' liabilities represent national insurance contributions not yet paid over.

Other creditors

'Other creditors' include any items that do not fit in anywhere else.

Accruals and deferred income

Accruals and deferred income, although shown together in accounts for Companies Act purposes, really consist of two quite different items.

Accruals are really only creditors by another name. A creditor is a liability which has been invoiced and is due for payment at the balance sheet date; an accrual is an item which has not been invoiced but where it is known that a liability has been incurred. Accruals can therefore be viewed as the opposite of prepayments. Many will be in respect of time-related expenses, such as electricity or gas, which are invoiced in arrears. Management accounts normally use the budgeted figure for time-related expenses as a substitute for the actual figure, with variances dealt with only on an occasional basis. Some companies also include as accruals, those invoices received after the year end and not booked in the bought ledger at the year end.

Deferred income is any income received *before* the balance sheet date which relates to a period after the balance sheet date. An example would be where a company invoices in advance for a time-related service, such as a maintenance contract or subscription. Another example would be government grants received before the year end but relating to a period after it. In management accounts, any deferred income should be highlighted and shown quite separately from creditors and accruals, with appropriate details given.

In some companies, instead of being included under the relevant category of creditors, accruals and deferred income are shown on a separate line of the balance sheet: this is an alternative presentation permitted by the Companies Act.

Other headings

There are also certain other headings for the analysis of creditors which do not apply to the Infallible group. These are:

- Payments received on account
- Bills of exchange payable
- Amounts owed to group undertakings
- Amounts owed to associated undertakings.

The heading *payments received on account* will be rarely used since such payments will be shown elsewhere. Payments on account of long-term work in progress are deducted from that figure in the balance sheet; but if payments received on account are greater than the amount of gross work in progress, the excess is included in this line. The heading does not include part payments from trade debtors. Those payments are deducted from debtors thereby reducing the amount of debtors shown in the balance sheet.

Bills of exchange are shown separately in the analysis of creditors. Bills of exchange are mainly used by companies for financing international trade.

Amounts owed to group undertakings or *to associated undertakings* are shown separately from all other creditors. In consolidated balance sheets these sums are self-cancelling and so do not appear.

Net current assets

Total creditors falling due within one year are deducted from total current assets (stocks, debtors, short-term investments and cash at bank and in hand) in the balance sheet to give a figure for *net current assets*. At this point a number of interesting calculations can be made which throw considerable light on the financial position of the business.

Current ratio

The current ratio is a measure of liquidity and gives an initial indication of a company's financial situation, at least in the short term. It is calculated as follows:

$$\frac{\text{Current assets}}{\text{Current liabilities}}$$

Example

The Infallible group's net current assets are as follows:

	£000
Stocks	2,970
Debtors	3,707
Investments	26
Cash at bank and in hand	3
	6,706
Less: current liabilities	(3,602)
Net current assets	3,104

and the current ratio is therefore:

$$\frac{6,706,000}{3,602,000} = 1.9$$

The comparable figure for the previous year was 1.8.

The reason that this ratio is so important is that, in order to stay in business, a company has to be able to pay its liabilities as they fall due. Unless it sells some of its fixed assets, in which case it may have to curtail the scale of its operations, or has a cash injection, the only places from which it can derive cash to pay its creditors are the items included in current assets. As it sells its stocks these will be replaced by debtors; when the debtors pay, the company will receive cash. If the company's total current assets are less than its current liabilities, where will the cash come from? If the two figures are about the same, the company may have to do some fancy juggling in order to keep all its creditors satisfied.

The ratio therefore ought to be substantially over 1.0 for a financially stable company. Trends are also important. Is the current ratio getting higher or lower? How stable is it compared with the company's competitors? What are their ratios?

Quick ratio

The quick ratio gives an even better understanding of a company's short-term financial stability. It is calculated by eliminating stocks from current assets, as follows:

$$\frac{\text{Current assets} - \text{stocks}}{\text{Current liabilities}}$$

This is often called the *acid test*. The period which it takes a company to sell stock and collect cash from its debtors can extend to several months. The company may not be able to survive that long without ready cash. Hence the quick ratio is the acid test for the company's short-term survival.

Example

Taking the Infallible group's figures, the quick ratio is 1.0 as calculated below:

$$\frac{6,706,000 - 2,970,000}{3,602,000} = 1.0$$

The comparable figure for the previous year was 0.9.

Again, trends are important, together with comparisons with other companies in the same sector. Nevertheless, most companies would aim for a quick ratio of at least 1.0. Of course, there *may* be other factors at work, and if a company has been happily continuing a business for many years with a quick ratio of much less than 1.0 it *may* be able to continue in business for the future.

But a downturn in its market sector or in the economy generally may put it out of business very quickly. If a company had a quick ratio of 1.2 two years ago, 1.0 last year and 0.8 this year, then steer well clear of it!

If you think that a company may be in financial difficulties, then the quick ratio is the key item to look at.

Finally, when looking at a company's current ratio and quick ratio, you should bear in mind its immediate capital expenditure programme and the possible need for increased working capital if its turnover is growing.

Working capital

Working capital is stocks plus trade debtors less trade creditors. You can see how much working capital is needed to support a given level of turnover by doing the following calculation:

$$\frac{\text{Working capital}}{\text{Turnover}} \times 100$$

The result is expressed as a percentage.

Example

Taking the Infallible group's figures, working capital represents 24 per cent of the year's turnover on continuing activities (including acquisitions) as calculated below:

$$\frac{2,970,000 + 3,243,000 - 1,942,000}{17,911,000} \times 100 = 24\%$$

If the company expects to increase its turnover by £1,000,000 next year, this would indicate a need for further working capital of £240,000. The comparable figure for the previous year was 26 per cent.

Foreign currencies

All borrowings, bank overdrafts and other creditors designated in foreign currency should be carefully monitored. In published accounts, such liabilities are usually translated into sterling at the exchange rate ruling at the balance sheet date.

Similar comments apply to liabilities designated in foreign currency as to current assets designated in foreign currency.

Provisions for liabilities and charges

A *provision* is an estimate of the amount of any liability or loss where it is known that the liability or loss is certain to be incurred, but where there is an element of doubt as to the actual amount. In such circumstances, the best estimate, made on a prudent basis, should be included in the accounts. Provisions may also include amounts set aside for any liabilities or losses which are likely to arise but which are not absolutely certain.

Provisions for liabilities and charges are analysed under three sub-headings in a note to the published balance sheet. The headings are:

● Pensions and similar obligations
● Taxation, including deferred taxation
● Other provisions.

Pensions and similar obligations is a heading which is particularly relevant to companies with defined benefit pension schemes (see Chapter 5).

Taxation, including deferred taxation will usually consist entirely of deferred taxation, which has been discussed earlier.

The Infallible group made a provision for the costs of closing down one of its divisions in 1993 which it included as an '*other provision*' in that year.

Contingent liabilities

Contingent liabilities are disclosed in a separate note, which will usually be found towards the end of the accounts.

Contingent liabilities are *potential* liabilities and are not included in the balance sheet. A contingent liability is one which may or may not arise, depending upon whether a specific event happens in the future. Such items are only taken up in the balance sheet when they crystallise into *actual* liabilities. If they are significant they will be disclosed in a note to the accounts, unless the possibility of any loss arising is very remote.

We have already encountered one example of a contingent liability in respect of debtors factored with recourse. Contingent liabilities may also include guarantees given by the business. In the event that a business was called upon to meet any of the guarantees, an actual liability would arise.

Some contingent liabilities depend upon the outcome of litigation. Management sometimes have a difficult job in satisfying the statutory obligation to disclose such contingent liabilities without showing their own assessment of the strength of their case to the other side in the litigation. The Infallible group's attempt is shown in Note 21 to the accounts.

It is very important to read the contingent liabilities note carefully. If it contains items which are large or unusual or do not appear to be closely related to the company's main activities, think very hard about the possible implications for the company if such items turned into actual liabilities. Quite possibly, the company could be driven out of business.

Other financial commitments

Where a company has entered into non-cancellable operating leases, it will show as a note to the accounts the sum which it is committed to pay over the next 12 months. Approximate details will also be given as to how long the leases have to run. From that you can deduce roughly how long the company will have to keep on making the payments. The Infallible group's commitments are set out in Note 20.

The notes to the accounts will also include details of any other financial commitments which a business has entered into which have not been reflected in the balance sheet.

All of this is potentially very important information. It will show the sort of commitments into which a company has entered and which it will have to honour whatever the results of its future trading.

CHAPTER 10

Balance Sheets – Capital and Reserves

Capital and reserves comprise the second section of a balance sheet. The total of a company's capital and reserves in this section will equal the total of its net assets in the first section.

Capital and reserves show the extent to which the net assets have been funded by the original capital introduced by shareholders, and by profits and surpluses generated by the business and retained by it. The latter are known as *reserves*.

Consolidated balance sheets may also have been funded partly by *minority interests*. Where a group of companies is not owned 100 per cent by the parent company, the minority interests in the balance sheet are the proportion of the group's net assets at the year end owned by outside shareholders.

The capital and reserves of the Infallible group are reproduced in Table 10.1.

Table 10.1 *Capital and reserves*

	1994 £000	1993 £000
Called up share capital	50	50
Share premium account	22	22
Revaluation reserve	552	–
Profit and loss account	3,436	2,453
	4,060	2,525
Minority interests	27	22
	4,087	2,547

Called up share capital

Called up share capital will be analysed further in published accounts, usually in a note, between the different classes of shares in issue. Different classes may have different rights.

The names given to different classes of share capital are *ordinary shares, preference shares* and *deferred shares*. Each share is allocated a nominal value which may or may not be the price at which it is issued by the company. This is because shares may be issued at a premium. There are legal restrictions on shares being issued at a discount. Share structures can become very complex and the particular characteristics of any class of shares will be defined by the company's articles of association.

The bulk of most companies' share capital is comprised of *ordinary shares*. Ordinary shares do not carry fixed dividends. Dividends can vary or be nil. On a winding up, ordinary shareholders are, however, entitled to any surplus capital remaining after all debts and obligations to most other classes of shareholder have been discharged. Most companies only have ordinary shares, but the characteristics of the other shares need to be appreciated.

Preference shares carry rights which have precedence over the rights of ordinary shares in respect of dividends or capital or both. Typically, preference shares are entitled to fixed dividends, but no more, and to a first claim on capital in a winding up.

Deferred shares are shares whose rights to dividends or capital or both are deferred to all or most other classes of shares, normally including ordinary shares.

For each class, the number and total nominal value of allotted shares will be given. The authorised share capital will also be noted. (The directors of a company are allowed to issue and allot shares only up to the company's authorised maximum for each class of shares, although the shareholders can increase this maximum by passing an appropriate resolution.)

A company will also give details if it has granted any *options* on any of its unissued share capital. It will state the number, description and amount of shares involved, the period during which the option is exercisable and the price to be paid under the option if it is exercised. Many large companies now give share options to their directors and senior executives, and it is interesting to see the incentives that have been given in this way. It is also worth seeing how far this will dilute existing shareholders' interests, although the quantum of share options is usually a very small proportion of the total number of shares in issue.

If any *fixed dividends* of a cumulative nature are in arrears this will also be stated in the notes. Arrears are likely to mean that the company has had a history of losses. Since payment of preference dividends takes precedence over payment of dividends on ordinary shares, significant arrears could indicate a long wait for any future dividends for ordinary shareholders.

Some shares may be *redeemable,* which means that they may be cancelled and the capital which they represent returned to the shareholders. If there are any redeemable shares in issue, the accounts will disclose the earliest and latest dates of redemption, and whether redemption is mandatory or at the company's option or the shareholders' option. They will also show the premium, if any, payable upon redemption. If mandatory redemption at a significant premium is imminent, this could make great financial demands upon a company.

If any shares have been allotted in the year, the details, together with the reasons for the issue, will be noted in the accounts. This may give an indication of the company's future intentions.

Reserves: non-distributable reserves

Reserves are either distributable or non-distributable. A *distributable reserve* is a reserve that there is nothing in law to prevent from being distributed to shareholders as dividends. A *non-distributable reserve* is a reserve which may not be so distributed.

Share premium account

If shares have been issued for a price which is higher than their nominal value, the excess of that price over the nominal value is included in the balance sheet as the *share premium account*. The share premium account is non-distributable and is treated for most purposes as being identical to share capital.

Revaluation reserve

Land and buildings are sometimes included in the accounts at a valuation higher than their original cost. The increase in value is not included in the profit and loss account but is shown as a revaluation reserve. It is non-distributable since it has not been realised.

If the property were to be sold and the reserve realised, there could be tax to pay. The amount of the potential tax liability (calculated after appropriate tax reliefs) may be shown as a note under the heading 'deferred taxation', although it is not usually included in the balance sheet. Sometimes properties can be sold without any tax liabilities arising because of a tax relief known as roll-over relief; in such cases the fact that no tax liability would arise will be stated.

The Infallible group has revalued its freehold land and buildings to £1,200,000, an increase of £552,000 over their previous book value. The figure of £552,000 is shown as a revaluation reserve.

Note 17 to the Infallible group's accounts states that, since the company has no intention of selling the property, it has not bothered to work out the tax that would be payable if it was sold! Many companies get away with similar notes.

Other reserves

If any of the three following reserves arise, they will be included under the heading of other reserves and details shown in the notes to the accounts:

- Capital redemption reserve
- Reserve for own shares
- Reserves provided for by the articles of association.

A *capital redemption reserve* arises where a company has redeemed or bought in part of its own share capital. It is created by transferring from profit and loss account a sum equivalent to the amount of capital redeemed. A capital redemption reserve is non-distributable and is treated for most purposes as being identical to share capital. The result is that the funds within the company which are treated as being capital remain unchanged.

Distributable reserve

Profit and loss account

This will show the accumulated undistributed profits to date after taking into account all taxation liabilities based on those profits. Many companies call this item *revenue reserve*. The *reconciliation of movement in shareholders' funds* (see Chapter 12) will show how the figure in the balance sheet links up with the retained profit for the year.

Unless the accounts say something different, a company's retained profits at the end of the year are distributable as dividends to shareholders. If there are any legal restrictions on paying them out a note will be made of how much is non-distributable. Retained profits shown in a group's consolidated balance sheet are not relevant for this purpose. Dividends can only be paid out of the retained profits in an individual company's balance sheet.

Shareholders' funds

The balance sheet will show a sub total of all the above items – called up share capital, share premium account, revaluation reserve and profit and loss account – which it will describe as *shareholders' funds*. The figure is equivalent to the net assets of the business (apart from any minority interests) and is also known as the *net worth* of the business.

One of the latest accounting standards requires accounts drawn up for periods ended on or after 22 June 1994 to analyse shareholders' funds between equity interests and non-equity interests.

In broad terms, that part of shareholders' funds described as *non-equity interests* will represent the proportion of the net assets of the company which is 'owned' by the holders of preference shares and redeemable shares. In the case of preference shares that will usually be merely the amount originally contributed to the company by the preference shareholders. In the case of redeemable shares the size of the figure will depend very much on the nature of the shares; it may include part of the growth in the company's assets since the shares were issued.

The balance of shareholders' funds will be described as *equity interests*. It will usually represent the proportion of the company's net assets which is 'owned' by the ordinary shareholders – the greatest part, in most cases. Where deferred shares have been issued, their share of the company's net assets will also normally be included as part of equity interests.

Since Infallible has only one class of shares – ordinary shares – all its shareholders' funds are shown as being equity interests.

Minority interests

The figure for minority interests represents the proportion of the net assets of subsidiaries owned by outside shareholders.

The Infallible group owns only 75 per cent of Dellboy Limited, the remaining 25 per cent of that company being owned by other shareholders. We may infer that minority interests of £27,000 at 31 December 1994 represent 25 per cent of the net assets of Dellboy Limited.

As with shareholders' funds, accounts drawn up for periods ended on or after 22 June 1994 will show an analysis of minority interests between equity and non-equity outside shareholders. In Infallible's case all the outside shareholders are ordinary shareholders – equity shareholders – and so the minority interests are shown as being minority equity interests.

Minority interests are sometimes included in the first section of the balance sheet.

Debt/equity ratio

Having reached the end of the balance sheet, it is now possible to calculate the debt/equity ratio. This shows the proportion of funds provided by third parties as compared with equity shareholders and minorities. It is usual to deduct any intangible assets from shareholders' funds. It is also usual to take only the funds attributable to equity shareholders. The calculation is as follows:

$$\frac{\text{Non-equity shareholders' funds} + \text{loans} + \text{bank overdraft}}{\text{Equity shareholders' funds} + \text{minority interest} - \text{intangible assets}}$$

Example
The Infallible group has no non-equity shareholders' funds: equity shareholders' funds of £4,060,000; total borrowings of £1,295,000; minority interests of £27,000; and intangible assets of £203,000.

Its debt/equity ratio is 33 per cent, calculated thus:

$$\frac{1,295,000}{4,060,000 + 27,000 - 203,000} \times 100 = 33\%$$

Some people might express this as a ratio of debt to equity of 1:3.

If the proportion of debt to equity is high, the company is said to be *highly geared*. A highly geared company is one which is financing its activities mainly by the use of other people's money (banks, debenture holders etc). A company with low gearing is financing its activities mainly by the use of the funds of its own ordinary shareholders. Some companies become highly geared in good times when they find it easy to borrow money to finance acquisitions etc. When the bad times come, they may have difficulty in borrowing more – or in servicing what they have borrowed already. High gearing is a danger sign when the economy hits a downturn, although it allows for rapid expansion when the economy is booming.

Net asset value
Net asset value is the value of assets attributable to each equity share. The assets are taken at their balance sheet value. It is calculated as follows:

$$\frac{\text{Equity shareholders' funds}}{\text{Number of equity shares issued}}$$

The Infallible group has equity shareholders' funds of £4,060,000 and called up ordinary share capital of £50,000. The net asset value of each share is therefore £81.

Return on capital employed

Return on capital employed measures the percentage return that a company is getting from the capital which it employs. One way to calculate it is as follows:

$$\frac{\text{Profit on ordinary activities before interest}}{\text{Capital employed in trading}} \times 100$$

Capital employed in trading is normally defined as shareholders' funds together with all borrowings, including bank overdrafts. Where there are significant minority interests and deferred liabilities these should be included. From these are deducted, where significant, any investments which produce investment income. This gives the capital employed in trading, that is the capital employed which is relevant to our definition of trading profit.

If capital employed has varied greatly between the start of the year and the end of the year, it would be sensible to take an average figure when making the calculation.

Example

The Infallible group's profit on ordinary activities before interest is £2,219,000. Its capital employed is £5,355,000 made up as follows:

	£000
Shareholders' funds	4,060
Borrowings	1,295
	5,355

Its return on capital employed is 41 per cent, calculated as follows:

$$\frac{2,219,000}{5,355,000} \times 100 = 41\%$$

Based on the average capital employed over the year the return on capital employed was 46 per cent.

If the return on capital employed, however defined, is less than the average interest rate paid on borrowings, something is seriously wrong. The capital employed might be better left in a bank on deposit! The Infallible group does not have this problem. Some companies do. It is difficult to see why anyone would want to provide them with capital.

CHAPTER 11

Cash Flow Statements

All companies which do not qualify for small-company exemptions (see Chapter 1) or which are not wholly owned subsidiaries will include a *cash flow statement* as part of their published accounts.

The aim of the cash flow statement is to translate into cash terms the profit for the year and other movements between the balance sheet at this year end and the balance sheet at the last year end. It shows the cash which the business has generated (or lost!) from its trading operations, the cash which it has obtained from outside sources, and the cash which it has spent on long-term assets.

There is a school of thought which believes that the cash flow statement is the most important document in a set of accounts. Subscribers to this school consider that cash, not profits, is the factor which determines whether a business can grow, whether it can survive hard times and whether it can pay dividends to its shareholders. Any non-accountants among them may wonder why accountants do not simply ignore the accruals concept and account for everything in cash terms in the first place!

The Infallible group's cash flow statement is set out in Table 11.1.

Let us look in detail at the way in which the cash flow statement is presented.

Cash flow from operations

The statement starts with a figure for cash generated from trading operations (before interest paid or received). This will not be the same figure as the profit shown in the profit and loss account which has to be adjusted for items which do not involve the inflow or outflow of cash. Depreciation is an example of one such item.

Table 11.1 *Cash flow statement*

	Note	1994 £000	1994 £000	1993 £000	1993 £000
CASH FLOW FROM OPERATIONS	25		1,646		1,278
RETURNS ON INVESTMENTS AND SERVICING OF FINANCE					
Interest paid		(162)		(242)	
Interest received		7		4	
Dividends on ordinary shares		(75)		(70)	
			(230)		(308)
TAXATION PAID			(375)		(310)
INVESTING ACTIVITIES					
Purchase of tangible fixed assets		(60)		(77)	
Purchase of intangible fixed assets		(205)		(1)	
Purchase of goodwill		(250)		–	
Purchase of listed investments		(4)		–	
Proceeds from disposal of tangible assets		54		29	
Proceeds from disposal of intangible assets		8		–	
			(457)		(49)
NET CASH INFLOW BEFORE FINANCING			584		611
FINANCING	26				
Repayment of debenture loan		(90)		(90)	
New bank loan		29		–	
Capital element of instalments paid under finance lease and hire purchase contracts		(128)		(90)	
NET CASH OUTFLOW FROM FINANCING			(189)		(180)
INCREASE IN CASH AND CASH EQUIVALENTS	27		395		431

Movements in stock and those movements in debtors and creditors which derive from trading activities are other examples.

These may require a word of explanation. Assume that a company spent a million pounds on stationery, two months before the year end, and that all the stationery was used by the balance sheet date but not paid for until after the year end. Profits would have decreased by a million pounds and creditors would have increased by the same sum. However, no cash would have left the business. An adjustment to the profit figure for the purpose of the cash flow statement is therefore called for. The increase of a million pounds in creditors is added to the figure for profit shown by the profit and loss account so as to give the correct cash flow effect.

Such adjustments are shown as part of a 'reconciliation' between the figure for cash flow from operations in the cash flow statement and the figure for profit shown in the profit and loss account. The reconciliation is shown in Note 25 to the Infallible group's accounts.

No adjustment is made for increases or decreases in creditors (or debtors) arising from transactions of a capital nature because capital items would not have affected the figure for profit in the first place. (This means that a reader of the accounts cannot check the reconciliation.)

Returns on investments and servicing of finance

The next section, headed returns on investment and servicing of finance, groups together interest paid on borrowings and dividends paid to shareholders (who provided the original capital or 'finance'). Together, these items comprise the cost of 'servicing' the finance used by the business. Interest received on any surplus cash balances which may have been invested is deducted. The resulting figure will show the net cash outflow (or inflow) from servicing the capital or finance which the company uses, after deducting any income generated from spare cash.

Taxation

The next line shows the amount of Corporation Tax which the company has paid (including Advance Corporation Tax). PAYE and Value Added Tax are not included here, having been deducted in arriving at the figure for cash flow from operations.

Investing activities

The next section deals with *investing activities*. Its aim is to show the amount spent on fixed assets and other capital items. (Any proceeds from the sale of fixed assets are deducted to give the net cash outflow.)

Unfortunately, the authors of the accounting standard which deals with cash flow statements hit a problem when it came to determining the treatment of fixed assets purchased under finance leases or hire-purchase agreements. As we explained in Chapter 7, such assets are treated in the accounts in the same way as assets which have been purchased using cash or ordinary bank borrowings, with the substance of the transaction – the purchase of a fixed asset – taking precedence over its form – a finance lease or hire-purchase agreement.

Unbelievably, the authors of the accounting standard on cash flow statements reversed this concept of 'substance over form', when laying down the rules for the treatment of such items in the cash flow statement. For the purposes of the cash flow statement, they have insisted that the form of the transaction should take precedence over its substance!

Any fixed assets bought under finance leases or hire-purchase agreements are therefore *excluded* from the *investing activities* section of the cash flow statement. One result of this is that where a company uses finance leases or hire-purchase agreements as a means of financing purchases, it is impossible to reconcile the figure shown for the purchase of fixed assets in the cash flow statement with the figure included in the main fixed asset note. The treatment followed in the cash flow statement is that each payment under a finance lease or hire-purchase contract is analysed between the 'interest' element (interest on the amount borrowed to finance the purchase) and the 'capital' element (that part of the instalment which repays part of the original amount borrowed). The capital element is included in the *financing* section of the cash flow statement and shown as the *capital element of finance lease instalments*. (The interest element is included as interest paid in the 'returns on investments and servicing of finance' section.)

The section on investing activities is also the place where the Infallible group shows the premium it paid for the goodwill of the trade of the business which it took over.

Financing

The aim of the *financing* section of the cash flow statement is to show cash flows arising from any changes in the way in which the business is financed. The issue of any new share capital is included here, as are any medium or long-term loans which have been raised. Conversely, the repayment of any loans or redeemable share capital is deducted. This heading also includes the capital element of any instalments paid on finance leases or hire purchase agreements, as we have seen. The section is totalled to show the net cash inflow (or outflow) from financing.

Increase in cash and cash equivalents

Generally, the total of the figures derived from all these different sections of the cash flow statement should equal the figure for the increase or decrease in the company's cash and bank balances.

Some companies, however, have specialised treasury functions and find it advantageous to make use of very short-term investments or borrowings rather than straightforward bank balances. Such very short-term investments or borrowings are termed *cash equivalents* for the purposes of the cash flow statement. Cash equivalents are defined as short-term, highly liquid investments which are readily convertible into known amounts of cash without notice, and which were within three months of maturity when acquired. They also include advances from banks repayable within three months from the date of the advance.

Cash flow statements group 'cash equivalents' with ordinary cash and bank balances.

Notes

A number of notes will be provided to the cash flow statement. The first, which we have mentioned earlier, will reconcile the figure shown for cash flow from operating activities in the cash flow statement to the figure shown for operating profit in the profit and loss account. Others show an analysis of cash and cash equivalents at the balance sheet date (with comparative figures for the previous balance sheet date), a note of the change in cash and cash equivalents during the year, and an analysis of changes in financing during the year.

Other than to see what items have been included as cash equivalents, there is little point in spending much time on the notes. In our view, they are there more for the benefit of accountants than for the readers. All they show is that things reconcile, although it is not always very easy to follow the reconciliation.

How to use the cash flow statement

Having looked at the constituent parts of the cash flow statement in detail, how are we to use the information presented? The most straightforward way is simply to read the cash flow statement as it is laid out. It will show how much cash has been generated from trading activities, the net costs of servicing borrowings and capital, taxation paid, how much the company has invested in new fixed assets (bearing in mind that any such assets 'bought' under finance leases and hire-purchase contracts will be excluded!), and changes in the long-term financing of the business (while also bearing in mind that this will include the capital elements of instalments on finance leases and hire-purchase agreements).

Another way of looking at the cash flow statement is to rearrange the figures: group all the cash inflows together, then the cash outflows. What proportion of the inflow is provided by trading and what proportion by new capital or long-term finance? Where does the business spend its cash? Is it on servicing its borrowings and capital or on investing for the future?

Compare the profit shown in the profit and loss account with the figure for cash flow from operations shown in the cash flow statement. How big is the difference? Is an apparently profitable business weak in terms of cash generation – are most of its profits just paper profits? Alternatively, does a business which shows only modest profits generate a steady stream of bankable cash?

If the profit and loss account and cash flow statement show a consistent picture – good profits and strong cash inflow – that will provide a measure of comfort. Sometimes, however, they are inconsistent. Some companies show a decent profit figure in their profit and loss account but their cash flow statements show that their trading operations actually lead to cash *outflows*. Do you understand why the differences arise? Do you believe the story told by the profit and loss account or the story told by the cash flow statement? It may pay to be a little wary.

Alternative presentation

The accounting standard dealing with cash flow statements permits companies to analyse further the net cash inflow from operating activities between cash received from customers, cash paid to suppliers, wages and salaries etc. This provides more detailed information about cash flows, but, in practice, very few companies give this information.

CHAPTER 12

Other Primary Statements

We mentioned in Chapter 1 that three comparatively new statements are now incorporated into annual financial accounts. They will usually be presented as *primary statements*, that is to say they will be given as much prominence as the profit and loss account, balance sheet and cash flow statement.

The three new statements are:

- Statement of total recognised gains and losses
- Reconciliation of movements in shareholders' funds
- Note of historical cost profits and losses.

Statement of total recognised gains and losses

The rationale behind this statement is that certain profits and losses – not very many, but an important few – are not passed through the profit and loss account. This is because either the Companies Act or an accounting standard requires (or permits) them to be excluded from the profit and loss account. Examples are:

- Book gains from upward revaluations of property
- Certain foreign currency gains and losses.

Previously, such items may have been hidden away in a note to the accounts. They are now collected together in the statement of total recognised gains and losses.

The Infallible group's statement of total recognised gains and losses is set out in Table 12.1.

Table 12.1 *Statement of total recognised gains and losses*

	1994	1993
	£000	£000
Profit for the financial year	1,358	657
Unrealised surplus on revaluation of freehold land and buildings	552	–
	1,910	657

The statement will always start with the profit for the financial year (before any dividends) as shown by the profit and loss account. It will then add any other profits or losses which have not passed through the profit and loss account – in the Infallible group's case, a surplus on the revaluation of land and buildings (which we described earlier as a book gain).

Finally, it will show the effect of any prior period adjustments which have not been charged or credited in arriving at the profit for the year shown by the profit and loss account. (The Infallible group does not have any.)

Prior period adjustments

Prior period adjustments represent retrospective adjustments to the profit of the previous year, or years. They may arise for one of two reasons.

The first reason is to correct a fundamental error in the previous figures. Full details will be spelt out and the previous year's figures will be restated. The normal comparatively minor errors and adjustments which arise in the preparation of the annual accounts do not fall into this category.

The second reason is where a business has changed an accounting policy. The change may have a significant impact on the level of reported profits. The current year's figures are calculated on the basis of the new policy and the previous year's figures are restated to show what they would have been had the new policy been used.

In both cases, the effect on the profits at the start of the year is shown separately as a prior period adjustment at the foot of the statement of total recognised gains and losses. The cumulative effect up to the start of the year before that may also be shown as a note.

Reconciliation of movements in shareholders' funds

The Infallible group's reconciliation of movements in shareholders' funds is set out in Table 12.2.

Table 12.2 *Reconciliation of movements in shareholders' funds*

	1994	1993
	£000	£000
Profit for the financial year	1,358	657
Dividends	125	75
	1,233	582
Other recognised gains and losses relating to the year (net)	552	–
Goodwill written off	(250)	–
	1,535	582
Opening shareholders' funds	2,525	1,943
Closing shareholders' funds	4,060	2,525

The aim of this statement is to reconcile shareholders' funds at the start of the year with shareholders' funds at the end of the year.

It does this by bringing together three things: the profit or loss shown by the profit and loss account; other profits or losses shown in the statement of total recognised gains and losses; and dividends paid. Then it does something which is likely to be confusing for the non-accountant (and for many accountants) – it adds or subtracts other movements in shareholders' funds which have not otherwise been accounted for.

What are these other movements? One example is new share capital subscribed for by the shareholders during the year. New share capital represents neither a profit nor loss so it would not be accounted for in either the profit and loss account or the statement of total recognised gains and losses.

Another example is goodwill which has been written off on the acquisition of a business. This is not accounted for through the profit and loss account and FRS 3, strangely, also prevents it from being accounted for through the statement of total recognised gains and losses. That is a very peculiar prohibition. We might have been excused for thinking that any business which pays money out and then immediately writes it off has recognised a loss. Not so, says FRS 3.

The Infallible group paid £250,000 during the year for the acquisition of the goodwill of a business and has written off this sum in the reconciliation of movements in shareholders' funds.

When all the figures have been added together, they are added to shareholders' funds at the start of the period (after any prior period adjustments have been deducted) to give the figure for shareholders' funds at the end of the period. It should be possible to agree this figure with the balance sheet.

In most cases, the reconciliation of shareholders' funds will tell a shareholder very little. He should, however, check to see whether or not any goodwill has been written off, since this is the only place in the accounts where it will be apparent. With that exception, the rest of the statement is merely a re-presentation of figures which already appear in the accounts. If you have seen them once, why bother to look at them again?

Note of historical cost profits and losses

The note of historical cost profits and losses is the third new statement introduced by FRS 3.

The note need only be included in cases where accounts have been prepared on something other than a 'pure' historical cost basis and where profits would have been significantly different if the accounts *had* been prepared on a 'pure' historical cost basis.

The note of historical cost profits and losses is supposed to be an abbreviated restatement of the profit and loss account as it would have appeared if no assets had been revalued. FRS 3 is full of restatements and re-analyses of parts of the accounts. The authors of FRS 3 take the view that users of the accounts are not interested in a single, unequivocal figure for the profit made by a company in a year, preferring instead a mass of different figures.

The authors of this book beg to differ. In our view, it mostly adds up to layer upon layer of confusion. We have difficulty in understanding just what use the information contained in the note of historical cost profits and losses is to most readers of accounts.

The Infallible group does not present a note of historical cost profits and losses, as the note is not relevant in its case.

You may note from this short chapter that we are not great enthusiasts for some of the changes which FRS 3 has introduced.

CHAPTER 13

Directors' Reports and Chairmen's Statements

Accompanying the annual published accounts will be a *directors' report*. Quoted companies will also publish a *chairman's statement* together with *a chief executive's review, or operating and financial review* or something similar. Non–quoted companies will rarely produce anything other than the directors' report.

Directors' report

There are a number of matters which are required by law to be dealt with in the directors' report. Perhaps the most important of these concern the principal activities of the business, its development during the year and its prospects. The directors' report is also the place to look for details of research and development, the market value of land and buildings, and particulars of the directors themselves.

Let us look at the main items which will be included.

Principal activities
The directors are required to state the principal activities of the company or group during the year, together with any significant changes which have been made to those activities in that period. It may well be interesting to read this information in conjunction with details of turnover and profits for different classes of business given in the notes to the accounts.

Business review
The directors must include a fair review of the development of the business during the financial year and of its position at the

end of the year. In the case of a group, this review encompasses all businesses carried on through subsidiary companies. The words 'fair review' are both broad and bland. It is open to directors to decide how much detail they wish to include. Many large quoted companies go into considerable detail in the chief executive's review and simply say in the directors' report that the business review is included in there. Many private companies say little more than that the performance of the business has been 'satisfactory'.

As well as dealing with the development of a business through the year, the directors' report will also give particulars of any important events which have occurred after the balance sheet date. If a company had bought or sold another business after the balance sheet date, that would certainly be an example of an event to be disclosed. Other than that, what is, and is not, an important event is open to judgment. This information also has to be given in a note to the accounts. Usually, it will be given once with a cross reference to it in the other document.

Future developments

The next requirement is for directors to indicate likely future developments in the business of the company, and, where appropriate, its subsidiaries. Here, we have moved away from the area of what has happened, which at least is factually based, to the area of what will happen, which, in the real world, is probably anyone's guess. All the directors can do is state what they intend to happen, or what they think is likely to happen. Accountants have developed stock phrases such as 'the directors expect to see continued growth in the foreseeable future' for use by smaller companies.

Research and development activities

The directors are required to give an indication of the research and development activities of the company and its subsidiaries.

The accounts themselves are required to give comparatively few details in this area. Only public companies and those private companies which are ten times bigger than the statutory definition of a medium-sized company have to disclose research and development expenditure for the year, as a note to the profit and loss account. It is a curious omission because one might think that, in the long run, the future success of many companies will depend on their success in this particular area, and that it is therefore the sort of information which shareholders ought to be given.

Fixed assets

Directors are required to note the nature of any significant changes in fixed assets during the year. Often, they will simply refer to the note on fixed assets in the main accounts.

They are also required to indicate, as precisely as they can, any substantial differences between the market value of interests in land owned by the business and the book value if, in their opinion, the difference is of such significance that it should be drawn to the attention of the shareholders. This information can be extremely useful to anyone trying to establish the real asset value of a business. Land and buildings bought decades ago are likely to have increased substantially in value but may not have been revalued in the balance sheet. On the other hand, land and buildings bought just before the property slump may have fallen in value.

Directors

The names of all persons who served as directors during the year will be shown. For those still directors at the end of the year, any interests which they had in the shares of the company (or any other group company) both at the end and beginning of the year (or the date when first appointed a director, if later) will be disclosed. Details do not have to be given by a wholly owned subsidiary for a person who is a director of both it and its parent company; in such instances, details are given only by the parent.

Dividends

Directors must state the amount of the dividend they recommend and the profit which they intend to transfer to reserves.

Employee information

Where the average number of UK employees was more than 250 during the year, the directors are required to state their policies on the employment of disabled persons and what actions they have taken during the year regarding employee involvement in the affairs of the business.

Political and charitable contributions

The separate totals of contributions for political and charitable purposes made during the year must be disclosed if together they exceed £200. If any individual donation of more than £200 has been made for political purposes, the name of the recipient and the amount must also be disclosed. Donations made to persons or parties outside the UK will not be shown. The requirement does not apply to wholly owned subsidiaries of UK parent companies.

Purchase of own shares

Appropriate details must be given by all companies which have purchased their own shares during the period.

Quoted companies

Certain other disclosures have to be made by listed companies:

- Directors have to state whether, so far as they are aware, the company is a 'close company' for taxation purposes.
- If any person other than a director has an interest of 3 per cent or more of any class of share capital carrying voting rights details have to be disclosed at a date not more than one month before the date of the notice of the shareholders' meeting at which the financial statements are to be presented.
- Details of any contract of significance between a group company and a corporate substantial shareholder. Particulars also have to be given of any contract for the provision of services to the company by a corporate substantial shareholder unless the provision of such services is the shareholder's principal business and the contract is not one of significance.
- Particulars of any authority given by the shareholders

enabling the company to purchase its own shares, if the authority is still in effect at the year end, must be disclosed.

● Any change in directors' interests between the end of the financial year and a date not more than one month before the date of the notice of the general meeting at which the accounts will be presented, must be shown.

● Further details concerning directors will also be shown.

Chairman's statement and chief executive's review of operations

All large quoted companies include a chairman's statement and many also include a chief executive's review, or something similar. These will usually be right at the front of the glossy brochure which is produced. They are usually distinguished by a very bright and attractive layout, with many photographs, in comparison with the drab presentation of the main accounts.

The information contained about the business can be extremely useful. The business is likely to be broken down into its constituent divisions with the activities, progress and future plans of each division set out in some detail. In particular, the products or services which lie at the centre of the business are likely to be fully described. For someone who wants to find out what the business actually does, rather than discover its financial results, these are the pages to head for. If you think that the products or services of the business are of a high quality, of great potential, or are based in growth areas, then this may be more important in its implications for the future than the results from the past set out in the accounts. Certainly, the key strategies adopted by a business are likely to be explicitly set out in such statements.

However, a note of caution should be sounded. Any figures contained in the statement are not audited and a chairman may well dwell on the more upbeat side of the business and pay less attention to areas of risk. In cases where a group has made an operating profit before exceptional items and interest costs, but has made a loss after those items have been charged, some chairmen have been known to give a certain emphasis to the first figure! Similarly, where the results for the year are analysed between continuing operations, acquisitions and discontinued operations, the figure which can be presented the most favourably will tend to be the one which receives the largest amount of comment.

Most statements and reviews will give great prominence to the names of some of the group's major products, especially those which are household names. These will very often bring a company's activities into sharp focus in the reader's eye. Keep in mind, though, that some household name products may actually represent quite minor businesses and may be only a small part of the group. In any event, many such products, with enviable reputations for quality, have in the past belonged to companies and groups which have proved to be financially unsound.

The names of key executives, other than group directors, who are responsible for the management of important divisions may also be given. This can be useful information if you are keeping a watching brief on an industry.

CHAPTER 14

Audit Reports

Auditors

Auditors have had a bad press recently.

The auditor's job – and it is a legal requirement imposed by the Companies Act – is to undertake an independent examination of the accounts prepared by the directors, and to give the shareholders an opinion as to whether those accounts show a true and fair view. That opinion is given in the audit report which is attached to the accounts issued to shareholders.

Auditors have a legal right of access to *all* the company's books and vouchers. They also have a legal right to require directors and other officers of the company to provide them with whatever information and explanations they request.

In theory, a company's auditors are appointed annually by a general meeting of the shareholders. In practice, the appointment is usually strongly influenced by the directors. Because of this, auditors have sometimes been accused of having too close an association with companies' executive directors. Quoted companies now have committees of non-executive directors – called audit committees – to liaise with the auditors in an attempt to limit the influence of the executive directors.

Most auditors are either Chartered Accountants or Certified Accountants and describe themselves as such at the foot of the audit report. They also add the words 'Registered Auditor' or 'Registered Auditors' to that description in order to show that they are registered to undertake company audits; only registered auditors are permitted to carry out such audits.

They generally work in partnerships which vary in size from two partners to several hundred. They may employ anything from a handful of staff to over 6,000 people.

Unqualified audit reports

If auditors believe that accounts are true and fair and have been properly prepared in accordance with the Companies Act, they issue a form of report called an *unqualified opinion*. This means that they have no reservations in saying that the accounts are true and fair.

The following is the standard form of wording:

AUDITORS' REPORT TO THE SHAREHOLDERS OF CECIL LIMITED

We have audited the accounts on pages 4–14 which have been prepared under the historical cost convention and the accounting policies set out on page 6.

Respective responsibilities of directors and auditors

As described on page 2 the company's directors are responsible for the preparation of financial statements. It is our responsibility to form an independent opinion, based on our audit, on those statements and to report our opinion to you.

Basis of opinion

We conducted our audit in accordance with Auditing Standards issued by the Auditing Practices Board. An audit includes examination, on a test basis, of evidence relevant to the amounts and disclosures in the accounts. It also includes an assessment of the significant estimates and judgements made by the directors in the preparation of the accounts, and of whether the accounting policies are appropriate to the company's circumstances, consistently applied and adequately disclosed.

We planned and performed our audit so as to obtain all the information and explanations which we considered necessary in order to provide us with sufficient evidence to give reasonable assurance that the accounts are free from material misstatement, whether caused by fraud or other irregularity or error. In forming our opinion we also evaluated the overall adequacy of the presentation of information in the accounts.

Opinion

In our opinion the accounts give a true and fair view of the state of the company's affairs as at 31 December 1994 and of its profit for the year then ended and have been properly prepared in accordance with the Companies Act 1985.

TRIED, TESTED & CO
Chartered Accountants
Registered Auditors
77 Audit Row
London EC1
31 January 1995

Let us look at this report in more detail.

Heading
The heading identifies to whom the report is addressed, namely the shareholders of Cecil Limited.

Introductory (unheaded) paragraph
The first paragraph of the audit report identifies by page numbers the accounts on which the auditors are reporting. This is quite important since, in the case of a large quoted company, the audited accounts may take up less than half of the large glossy brochure sent to shareholders. Any information which falls outside the numbered pages referred to in the audit report has *not* been audited.

The directors' report, chairman's statement and chief executive's review are not audited, although auditors are required by law to say if anything in the directors' report is inconsistent with the audited accounts. Other than that, they have no obligation, and no rights, to comment in their audit report on any material in the brochure except the accounts. They do have a right, however, to speak at shareholders' meetings on any business which concerns them as auditors.

Respective responsibilities of directors and auditors
This paragraph is an attempt by auditors to remind people that it is the directors, not the auditors, who have prepared the accounts. It refers to the statement of directors' responsibilities, an example

of which is set out below, which will usually be found at the end of the directors' report or just before the audit report.

STATEMENT OF DIRECTORS' RESPONSIBILITIES

Company law requires the directors to prepare accounts for each financial year which give a true and fair view of the state of the company's affairs and of its profit or loss for that period. In preparing those financial statements, the directors are required to:

- select suitable accounting policies and apply them consistently;
- make judgements and estimates that are reasonable and prudent;
- state whether applicable accounting standards have been followed, subject to any material departures disclosed and explained in the accounts;
- prepare the accounts on a going concern basis unless it is inappropriate to presume that the company will continue in business.

The directors are responsible for keeping proper accounting records which disclose with reasonable accuracy at any time the financial position of the company and to enable them to ensure that the financial statements comply with the Companies Act 1985. They are also responsible for safeguarding the assets of the company and hence for taking reasonable steps for the prevention and detection of fraud and other irregularities.

Let us resume our look at the audit report.

Basis of opinion

The basis of opinion paragraph highlights the fact that auditors examine the transactions underlying the accounts on a test basis only; they do not check them 100 per cent. It again stresses that the directors will have made estimates and exercised their judgement when preparing the accounts and when choosing accounting policies. Unless stated otherwise, it can be assumed that the auditors concur with the directors' accounting judgements – but not necessarily with their business judgements!

Opinion

The final paragraph of the auditors' report says, without any reservations, that, in the auditors' opinion, the accounts are true and fair and have been properly prepared in accordance with the Companies Act.

The opinion paragraph refers only to the profit and state of affairs. Nevertheless, the Auditing Practices Board, which drafted the new form of wording, has stated that the wording also covers both the cash flow statement and the statement of total recognised gains and losses unless something is said to the contrary. In the interests of clarity, it would be better to spell this out and, to their credit, some firms of auditors have decided to do so.

Termination

The report ends by giving the name and address of the auditors. (Some large firms of auditors consider themselves to be so well known and prestigious that they merely give their address as 'London'.)

Lastly, the report is dated. This is the date on which the audit report was signed. The date can be significant. Auditors will not have considered any events occurring *after* that date which might have given them additional information on balance sheet assets and liabilities. Watch out for accounts containing audit reports dated months before you receive them.

Fundamental uncertainties

Sometimes the directors have to make judgements in the accounts about the outcome of uncertain events and the judgements are so fundamental to the view given by the accounts that, if they turn out to have been wrong, the accounts would be seriously misleading.

In such cases, even though the auditors agree that, on the balance of probabilities, the directors are right, they think it necessary to highlight the relevant area of uncertainty in their report by including a paragraph (headed 'Fundamental uncertainty') immediately after the 'Basis of opinion' paragraph. They conclude by saying 'our opinion is not qualified in this respect'. The aim is simply to put the reader on guard that events may unfold which mean that the treatment adopted in the accounts may turn out, in retrospect, to have been inappropriate.

An example of auditors treating readers of accounts like adults? Or just another example of auditors trying to have it both ways?

We give an example below of disclosure of a fundamental uncertainty, the uncertainty in this case being whether or not the company is a going concern.

Fundamental uncertainty

In forming our opinion, we have considered the adequacy of the disclosure made in the accounts concerning the possible outcome of negotiations for additional finance to replace an existing loan of £100,000 which is repayable on 30 June 1995. The accounts have been prepared on a going concern basis, the validity of which depends on future funding being available. The accounts do not include any adjustments that would result from a failure to obtain funding. Details of the circumstances relating to this fundamental uncertainty are described in Note 16. Our opinion is not qualified in this respect.

If the auditors had disagreed that, on the basis of probabilities, the company was a going concern, they would, or should, have said so.

Qualified opinions arising from disagreement about accounting treatment

There are occasions on which auditors will disagree with the treatment of a particular item in the accounts but are happy with the accounts in other respects. In that case, they will head the final paragraph of their report 'Qualified opinion arising from disagreement about accounting treatment'.

In such an instance, they use the words 'except for' when giving their opinion. First, they set out the relevant circumstances. Second, they will say that 'except for' the particular matter concerned, the accounts give a true and fair view. A frequent example of an 'except for' opinion occurs when accounts have been prepared on a basis which does not comply with an applicable accounting standard.

Incidentally, if a company omitted to produce a cash flow statement, the accounts would also receive an 'except for' opinion with the paragraph headed 'Qualified opinion arising from omission of cash flow statement'.

Adverse opinion

If the matter with which the auditors disagree was so material or pervasive that they concluded that the accounts were seriously misleading, they would issue an *adverse opinion*. They would say that, in their opinion, the accounts do *not* give a true and fair view. The final paragraph of the report would then be headed 'Adverse opinion'.

As with the previous example, the auditors would first summarise the relevant circumstances. They would then say something along the lines of, 'In view of the effect of [the matters in question], in our opinion the accounts do not give a true and fair view . . .'.

That is the strongest qualification possible. The auditors are saying that the accounts are fundamentally wrong. Any accounts where the auditors have given an adverse opinion are more or less worthless. Such qualifications are rare, perhaps because the threat of one leads companies to change the accounts so as to avoid it.

Limitation on scope of audit

There will be occasions when the scope of the auditors' work has been limited in such a way that they have been prevented from obtaining sufficient audit evidence to enable them to express an unqualified opinion. Such limitations may have arisen because the directors acted illegally in not making all the accounting records available to the auditors; or they may have prevented them from carrying out a test which they wanted to carry out. Limitations could also arise as a result of factors outside the control of either the auditors or directors, eg a fire or computer breakdown.

In either event, the auditors will expand the 'Basis of opinion' section of their report, saying that they conducted their audit in accordance with Auditing Standards issued by the Auditing Practices Board 'except that the scope of our work was limited as explained below'. The circumstances of the limitation will then be summarised. They then have two options.

Qualified opinion arising from limitation in audit scope

If they believe that, while the limitation is material, it is not so material or pervasive that they are unable to give any opinion at all, the auditors will issue an opinion headed 'Qualified opinion arising from limitations in audit scope' along the following lines:

> 'Except for any adjustments that might have been found to be necessary had we been able to obtain audit evidence [about the matters where the scope of their work has been limited], in our opinion the financial statements give a true and fair view . . .'.

Since auditors are required by the Companies Act to make a statement where they have been unable to obtain all the information and explanations that they considered necessary for the purposes of their audit, and are also required to make a statement where, in their view, proper accounting records have not been kept, they will go on to say:

> 'In respect alone of the limitation of our work relating to [the matters concerned]
> - we have not obtained all the information and explanations that we considered necessary for the purposes of our audit; and
> - we were unable to determine whether proper accounting records had been maintained.'

Disclaimer of opinion

Occasionally, auditors will conclude that the limitation on the scope of their work is so material or so pervasive that they are unable to give any opinion at all. They will then head the final paragraph of their report (the opinion paragraph) 'Opinion: disclaimer on view given by accounts' and will say, 'Because of the possible effect of the limitation in evidence available to us, we are unable to form an opinion as to whether the accounts give a true and fair view . . .'.

They will add, nevertheless, that 'In all other respects, in our opinion the accounts have been properly prepared in accordance with the Companies Act'. This rather strange sentence will appear because auditors remain required by law to report on compliance with the Companies Act in other respects, even when they do not think that the accounts give a true and fair view. It is not much of a comfort.

Group accounts

Audit reports on group accounts will refer to the state of affairs of both the company and the group at the balance sheet date because group accounts contain two balance sheets, one for the parent company and one for the group. However, they will refer only to the profit of the group, not to the company, since separate figures for the parent company are not included in the accounts.

Fraud

One final point needs to be made concerning the audit report. Auditors are only concerned with ensuring that accounts are free from material misstatement. If a fraud, or other irregularity, was so material as to seriously distort the reported profit for the year, or the balance sheet at the end of the year, auditors would expect to find out about it in the course of their audit work. If they did not, their audit opinion on the truth and fairness of the accounts would rest on shaky ground.

The responsibility for preventing and detecting fraud lies, however, with the directors. It is the directors' responsibility to set up an appropriate system of financial and other controls to achieve this. (Remember that the final paragraph in the Statement of Directors' Responsibilities acknowledges that point.) In a large company a fraud can involve a sum of money which is substantial for an individual but which may nevertheless be immaterial from the point of view of the accounts as a whole. Auditors are therefore clear in their own minds that they do not have a duty specifically to search for what – from their point of view – may be immaterial frauds. The general public does not always share this view.

Quoted companies' half-yearly figures

Quoted companies are required to issue half-yearly summary profit and loss accounts to shareholders. These figures will be reviewed by the auditors but not audited. The auditors will ask the company's management questions about how the figures were arrived at, look at whether they seem to make sense and find out whether the accounting policies used are the same as those in the last audited accounts. They will not, however, try to verify the assets and liabilities and will not carry out any audit tests.

Small companies

Very small private companies are now completely exempt from the requirement to have their accounts audited. A company qualifies if:

● its turnover for the year is not more than £90,000;
● its gross assets are not more than £1,400,000;
● it qualifies as a small company (see page 23) in all other respects; and
● it is not part of a group and is not subject to a statute-based regulatory regime, such as the Financial Services Act 1986.

If its turnover is between £90,000 and £350,000 (and the other conditions hold good) then, while it is still exempt from an audit it has, nevertheless, to have an accountant's report attached to its accounts. The report has to be made by a qualified practising accountant and has to say:

● whether the accounts are in agreement with the underlying accounting records;
● whether they have been drawn up in a manner consistent with the provisions of the Companies Act; and

● whether the company satisfied the conditions for exemptions from audit.

Any shareholder who owns 10 per cent or more of any class of the company's share capital can veto either of the above arrangements and insist that the accounts are fully audited.

The original idea behind all of this was to do away with some of the regulations which applied to small companies. It is certainly a step in the right direction – but a very small one. The main draw-back, which applies to companies which fall into each of the two categories, is that their accounts continue to have to comply with all the detailed provisions set out in the Companies Act. That means that, in practice, even companies with turnovers of £90,000 or less will continue to have to use the services of a qualified accountant – since only qualified accountants fully understand the Companies Act!

Since companies will probably also continue to need tax advisers – usually accountants – to guide them through the UK's highly complex and complicated tax legislation and to argue their case with the Inland Revenue, we suggest that few small companies will see large reductions in their accountancy fees.

CHAPTER 15

Checklist 1 – Questions

Try asking these questions when someone hands you – or sends you – a set of accounts.

General questions?

1. What business is the company in?
2. What matters am I going to decide, if any, on the basis of reading these accounts?
3. What information do I therefore need, and how precise does it have to be?
4. Are the accounts audited? If so, is the audit report unqualified? (If the report is qualified, consider the implications regarding the trustworthiness of the accounts.)
5. Do the audited accounts agree with the management accounts? (If not, what are the differences, and why?)
6. How out of date are the figures?

The overall impression

7. Which are the biggest figures in the accounts? Look at these first.
8. Are the figures what I would expect them to be? If not, why not?
9. What are the trends?

Are any figures misleading?

10. How is goodwill treated (where applicable)? What would be the effect if it was treated differently?
11. Are there any brand names in the balance sheet? What would be the effect if they were written off?
12. Are there any unusual accounting policies?

Is the company profitable?

13. What is the gross profit percentage?
14. What is the net profit margin on sales?
15. What is the return on capital?
16. What are the dividends?
17. How much do the directors pay themselves?

How good is its financial management?

18. What is the stockholding period?
19. How quickly does it collect its debtors?
20. How quickly does it pay its creditors?

Whose money is it using?

21. What is the capital structure?
22. What is the borrowing structure?
23. What is the interest cover?

Will the company still be trading next month?

24. What is the current asset ratio?
25. What is the quick asset ratio?
26. How much does it owe the bank?
27. What contingent liabilities does the business have? Are they usual for the trade? What would happen if they became real liabilities?

And after that?

28. What is the future capital expenditure programme?
29. What financial commitments does it have?
30. What additional working capital will it need if it expands?

CHAPTER 16

Checklist 2 –
Where to Find What

We set out below where to look in the accounts to find information which will not hit you in the eye when you look at the profit and loss account or balance sheet.

Subject	Where to find it
Bank overdraft	Note to the accounts (creditors)
Brand names	Note to the accounts (accounting policies)
Capital commitments	Note to the accounts (usually towards the end)
Charitable donations	Directors' report
Contingent liabilities	Note to the accounts (usually towards the end)
Depreciation rate	Note to the accounts (accounting policies)
Depreciation charge	Note to the accounts (fixed assets)
Different classes of business	Note to the accounts (turnover)
Directors	
– names	Directors' report
– shareholdings	Directors' report
– remuneration	Note to the accounts
– transactions with the company	Note to the accounts, if applicable
– loans to directors	Note to the accounts, if applicable
Employee numbers and analysis	Note to the accounts (usually towards the end)
EPS (quoted companies)	Note to the accounts
Events after the year end	Directors' report and note to the accounts

Future financial commitments	Note to the accounts (usually towards the end)
Future developments	Directors' report
Goodwill	Note to the accounts (accounting policies)
Land and buildings	Note to the accounts (tangible fixed assets) and directors' report
Long-term borrowing details	Note to the accounts (creditors)
Markets	Note to the accounts (turnover)
Names of subsidiaries	Note to the accounts (fixed asset investments)
Pension costs	Note to the accounts (including accounting policies)
Plant and machinery	Note to the accounts (tangible fixed assets)
Political contributions	Directors' report
Principal activities	Directors' report
Research and development	Directors' report and (for large companies) note to the accounts
Sales analysis	Note to the accounts (turnover)
Stocks	Note to the accounts (including accounting policies)
Trade creditors	Note to the accounts
Trade debtors	Note to the accounts
Trading review	Directors' report (chairman's statement or chief executive's review for quoted companies)
Ultimate parent company	Note to the accounts

Appendix

INFALLIBLE LIMITED

31ST DECEMBER 1994

INFALLIBLE LIMITED
REPORT OF THE DIRECTORS

The directors present their report and the group financial statements for the year ended 31st December 1994.

DIRECTORS
The directors who served during the year were :
A T Green
Mrs B White
P L Stephens
W A Brass
W A Brass retires by rotation and, being eligible, offers himself for re-election.

PRINCIPAL ACTIVITY AND BUSINESS REVIEW
The principal activity of the group throughout the year continued to be the manufacture and distribution of colour designs.

The directors continued to pursue their policy of closing unprofitable divisions and acquiring businesses in the colour design field with higher growth prospects for the future. The decision to terminate the activities of the Pink Division (which had been taken in the previous financial year with a provision against the expected loss on termination having been made in that year's accounts) was implemented during the course of the year. In March 1994, the group acquired the trade, patents and trade marks of Jeremiah Mauve. This trade now operates as a separate division within the group and the directors believe that it has prospects for considerable expansion.

The results for the year and the financial position at the year end were considered satisfactory by the directors who also expect continued growth in turnover and profitability in the foreseeable future.

FIXED ASSETS
Details of changes in fixed assets are shown in Notes 9 and 10 to the financial statements.

The freehold land and buildings were revalued to their open market value for existing use at 31st December 1994.

DIRECTORS' INTERESTS
The directors had the following interests in the shares of the company at the beginning and end of the year:

A T Green	15,000
Mrs B White	15,000
P L Stephens	5,000
W A Brass	2,000

None of the directors held shares in any other group company at either date.

RESEARCH AND DEVELOPMENT
The group continued its policy of investment in research and development in order to maintain a competitive position in the market.

1

154   UNDERSTANDING COMPANY ACCOUNTS

CHARITABLE CONTRIBUTIONS
The group made charitable contributions during the year of £2,400. No political contributions were made.

DISABLED EMPLOYEES
The group gives full consideration to applications for employment from disabled persons where the requirements of the job can be adequately fulfilled by the handicapped or disabled. Similarly, it is the group's policy to continue to provide employment and career development opportunities to any existing employee who becomes disabled.

EMPLOYEE INVOLVEMENT
Within the bounds of commercial confidentiality, information is disseminated to all members of staff about matters that affect the progress of the group and are of interest and concern to them as employees by means of a quarterly group newsletter and by regular meetings between local management and employees.

DIVIDENDS AND TRANSFER TO RESERVES
The directors paid an interim dividend of £1 per share (1993: £1) and recommend an increased final dividend of £1.50 per share (1993: 50p).

It is proposed to transfer the retained profit for the year of £1,233,000 to reserves.

FUTURE DEVELOPMENTS
Approval has been given for the construction of an extension to the factory which is expected to be completed by the summer of 1996. This will double the group's production capacity and allow for further future growth.

AUDITORS
Tried, Tested & Co. have expressed their willingness to continue in office as auditors and a resolution for their reappointment will be proposed at the forthcoming Annual General Meeting.

DIRECTORS' RESPONSIBILITIES FOR THE ACCOUNTS
Company law requires the directors to prepare accounts for each financial year which give a true and fair view of the state of affairs of the company and of the group and of the profit or loss of the group for that period. In preparing those accounts the directors are required to:

- select suitable accounting policies and then apply them consistently;
- make judgements and estimates that are reasonable and prudent;
- state whether applicable accounting standards have been followed, subject to any material departures disclosed and explained in the accounts;
- prepare the accounts on the going concern basis unless it is inappropriate to presume that the company and group will continue in business.

The directors confirm that they have complied with the above requirements in preparing the accounts.

2

The directors are responsible for keeping proper accounting records which disclose with reasonable accuracy at any time the financial position of the company and of the group and to enable them to ensure that the accounts comply with the Companies Act 1985. They are also responsible for safeguarding the assets of the company and of the group and hence for taking reasonable steps for the prevention and detection of fraud and other irregularities.

on behalf of the Board
A T GREEN
Chairman

31st January 1995

3

AUDITORS' REPORT
TO THE SHAREHOLDERS OF INFALLIBLE LIMITED

We have audited the accounts on pages 5 to 20 which have been prepared under the historical cost convention (as modified by the revaluation of certain fixed assets) and the accounting policies set out on pages 10 and 11.

Respective responsibilities of directors and auditors
As described on page 2 the company's directors are responsible for the preparation of accounts. It is our responsibility to form an independent opinion, based on our audit, on those accounts and to report our opinion to you.

Basis of opinion
We conducted our audit in accordance with Auditing Standards issued by the Auditing Practices Board. An audit includes examination, on a test basis, of evidence relevant to the amounts and disclosures in the accounts. It also includes an assessment of the significant estimates and judgements made by the directors in the preparation of the accounts, and of whether the accounting policies are appropriate to the group's circumstances, consistently applied and adequately disclosed.

We planned and performed our audit so as to obtain all the information and explanations which we considered necessary in order to provide us with sufficient evidence to give reasonable assurance that the accounts are free from material misstatement, whether caused by fraud or other irregularity or error. In forming our opinion we also evaluated the overall adequacy of the presentation of information in the accounts.

Opinion
In our opinion the accounts give a true and fair view of the state of affairs of the company and of the group as at 31st December 1994 and of the profit of the group for the year then ended and have been properly prepared in accordance with the Companies Act 1985.

TRIED, TESTED & CO
Chartered Accountants
Registered Auditors

77 Audit Row
London EC1

31st January 1995

INFALLIBLE LIMITED
CONSOLIDATED PROFIT AND LOSS ACCOUNT
FOR THE YEAR ENDED 31ST DECEMBER 1994

	Notes	1994 £000	1994 £000	1993 £000
TURNOVER				
Continuing operations				
ongoing		15,508		14,505
acquisitions		2,403		–
		17,911		14,505
Discontinued operations		1,147		2,367
	2		19,058	16,872
Cost of sales	3		6,729	6,320
Gross profit			12,329	10,552
Net operating expenses	3		10,094	9,218
OPERATING PROFIT				
Continuing operations				
ongoing		2,331		1,361
acquisitions		2		–
		2,333		1,361
Discontinued operations		(98)		(27)
			2,235	1,334
Provision for loss on operations to be discontinued		–		70
Loss on termination of discontinued operations	4	86		–
Less: 1993 provision		70		–
			16	70
PROFIT ON ORDINARY ACTIVITIES BEFORE INTEREST			2,219	1,264
Interest payable less receivable	5		144	243
PROFIT ON ORDINARY ACTIVITIES BEFORE TAXATION			2,075	1,021
Tax on profit on ordinary activities	7		712	361
PROFIT ON ORDINARY ACTIVITIES AFTER TAXATION			1,363	660
Minority equity interests			5	3
PROFIT FOR THE FINANCIAL YEAR			1,358	657
Dividends	8		125	75
RETAINED PROFIT			1,233	582

5

INFALLIBLE LIMITED
CONSOLIDATED BALANCE SHEET
AS AT 31ST DECEMBER 1994

	Notes	1994 £000	1994 £000	1993 £000	1993 £000
FIXED ASSETS					
Intangible assets	9	203		14	
Tangible assets	10	1,508		862	
			1,711		876
CURRENT ASSETS					
Stocks	12	2,970		2,907	
Debtors	13	3,707		2,760	
Investments	14	26		22	
Cash at bank and in hand		3		30	
		6,706		5,719	
CREDITORS – Amounts falling due within one year	15	3,602		3,258	
NET CURRENT ASSETS			3,104		2,461
TOTAL ASSETS LESS CURRENT LIABILITIES			4,815		3,337
CREDITORS – Amounts falling due after more than one year	16	707		720	
PROVISIONS FOR LIABILITIES AND CHARGES	17	21		70	
			728		790
			4,087		2,547
CAPITAL AND RESERVES					
Called up share capital	18		50		50
Share premium account			22		22
Revaluation reserve			552		–
Profit and loss account			3,436		2,453
Equity shareholders' funds			4,060		2,525
Minority equity interests			27		22
			4,087		2,547

A T GREEN – Director
Approved by the board on 31st January 1995

INFALLIBLE LIMITED
BALANCE SHEET
AS AT 31ST DECEMBER 1994

	Notes	1994 £000	1994 £000	1993 £000	1993 £000
FIXED ASSETS					
Intangible assets	9	197		5	
Tangible assets	10	1,508		862	
Investments	11	219		219	
			1,924		1,086
CURRENT ASSETS					
Stocks	12	2,914		2,767	
Debtors	13	3,243		2,462	
Investments	14	26		22	
Cash at bank and in hand		3		5	
		6,186		5,256	
CREDITORS – Amounts falling due within one year	15	3,515		3,205	
NET CURRENT ASSETS			2,671		2,051
TOTAL ASSETS LESS CURRENT LIABILITIES			4,595		3,137
CREDITORS – Amounts falling due after more than one year	16	707		720	
PROVISION FOR LIABILITIES AND CHARGES	17	21		70	
			728		790
			3,867		2,347
CAPITAL AND RESERVES					
Called up share capital	18		50		50
Share premium account			22		22
Revaluation reserve			552		–
Profit and loss account			3,243		2,275
Equity shareholders' funds			3,867		2,347

A T GREEN – Director
Approved by the board on 31st January 1995

7

INFALLIBLE LIMITED
YEAR ENDED 31ST DECEMBER 1994
STATEMENT OF TOTAL RECOGNISED GAINS AND LOSSES

	1994 £000	1993 £000
Profit for the financial year	1,358	657
Unrealised surplus on revaluation of freehold land and buildings	552	–
	1,910	657

RECONCILIATION OF MOVEMENTS IN SHAREHOLDERS' FUNDS

	1994 £000	1993 £000
Profit for the financial year	1,358	657
Dividends	(125)	(75)
	1,233	582
Other recognised gains and losses relating to the year (net)	552	–
Goodwill written off	(250)	–
	1,535	582
Opening shareholders' funds	2,525	1,943
Closing shareholders' funds	4,060	2,525

INFALLIBLE LIMITED
CONSOLIDATED CASH FLOW STATEMENT
FOR THE YEAR ENDED 31ST DECEMBER 1994

	Notes	1994 £000	1994 £000	1993 £000	1993 £000
CASHFLOW FROM OPERATIONS	25		1,646		1,278
RETURNS ON INVESTMENTS AND SERVICING OF FINANCE					
Interest paid		(162)		(242)	
Interest received		7		4	
Dividends on ordinary shares		(75)		(70)	
NET CASH OUTFLOW FROM INVESTMENTS AND SERVICING OF FINANCE			(230)		(308)
TAXATION PAID			(375)		(310)
INVESTING ACTIVITIES					
Purchase of tangible fixed assets		(60)		(77)	
Purchase of intangible fixed assets		(205)		(1)	
Purchase of goodwill		(250)		–	
Purchase of listed investments		(4)		–	
Proceeds from disposal of tangible assets		54		29	
Proceeds from disposal of intangible assets		8		–	
NET OUTFLOW FROM INVESTING ACTIVITIES			(457)		(49)
NET CASH INFLOW BEFORE FINANCING			584		611
FINANCING	26				
Repayment of debenture loan		(90)		(90)	
New bank loan		29		–	
Capital element of instalments paid under finance lease and hire purchase contracts		(128)		(90)	
NET CASH OUTFLOW FROM FINANCING			(189)		(180)
INCREASE IN CASH AND CASH EQUIVALENTS	27		395		431

9

INFALLIBLE LIMITED
NOTES TO THE CONSOLIDATED ACCOUNTS
FOR THE YEAR ENDED 31ST DECEMBER 1994

1. ACCOUNTING POLICIES

(a) **Basis of preparation**

The accounts are prepared under the historical cost convention as modified by the revaluation of certain fixed assets and in accordance with applicable accounting standards.

(b) **Basis of consolidation**

The group accounts consolidate the accounts of Infallible Limited and its subsidiary undertakings all of which are drawn up to 31st December each year.

(c) **Deferred taxation**

Deferred taxation is provided on the liability method on all timing differences which are expected to reverse in the future without being replaced, calculated at the rate at which it is expected that taxation will be payable.

(d) **Depreciation**

Depreciation of fixed assets is provided at the following annual rates by the straight line method:

Freehold land	nil
Freehold buildings	2%
Plant and machinery	20%
Fixtures and equipment	15%
Motor vehicles	25%
Patents and trade marks	10%

(e) **Foreign currencies**

Transactions in foreign currencies are recorded at the rate ruling at the date of the transaction. Monetary assets and liabilities denominated in foreign currency are retranslated at the rate of exchange ruling at the balance sheet date. All exchange differences are taken to the profit and loss account.

(f) **Goodwill**

Purchased goodwill is written off directly against reserves.

(g) **Leasing and hire purchase commitments**

Assets held under finance leases and hire purchase contracts are capitalised in the balance sheet and are depreciated over their useful lives. The interest element of the rental obligations is charged to the profit and loss account over the period of the lease and represents a constant proportion of the balance of capital repayments outstanding.

Rentals paid under operating leases are dealt with in the profit and loss account as incurred.

(h) **Pensions**

The group operates a defined benefit pension scheme. The assets of the scheme are held in a separate trustee-administered fund. Contributions to the scheme are charged to the profit and loss account so as to spread the pension costs over employees' expected working lives with the group.

INFALLIBLE LIMITED
NOTES TO THE CONSOLIDATED ACCOUNTS
FOR THE YEAR ENDED 31ST DECEMBER 1994

1. ACCOUNTING POLICIES – continued

(i) **Research and development**
Research and development expenditure is written off in the year in which it is incurred.

(j) **Stocks**
Stocks are stated at the lower of cost and net realisable value. Cost is determined on a first in, first out basis. The cost of work in progress and finished goods comprises materials, direct labour and attributable production overheads. Net realisable value is based on estimated selling price less any further costs which are expected to be incurred to completion and disposal.

(k) **Turnover**
Turnover represents the invoiced value of goods sold, excluding sales between group companies, value added tax and trade discounts.

2. GEOGRAPHICAL ANALYSIS OF TURNOVER

	1994	1993
	£000	£000
United Kingdom	16,818	15,191
North America	2,240	1,681
	19,058	16,872

3. COST OF SALES AND NET OPERATING EXPENSES

	1994			1993		
	Continuing	Discontinued	Total	Continuing	Discontinued	Total
	£000	£000	£000	£000	£000	£000
Cost of sales	6,152	577	6,729	5,252	1,068	6,320
Net operating expenses:						
Distribution costs	4,073	417	4,490	3,440	704	4,144
Administrative expenses	5,375	251	5,626	4,452	622	5,074
Other operating income	(22)	–	(22)	–	–	–
	9,426	668	10,094	7,892	1,326	9,218

The total figures for continuing operations in 1994 include the following amounts relating to acquisitions: cost of sales £1,118,000; distribution costs £351,000; administrative expenses £954,000; and other operating income £22,000.

4. EXCEPTIONAL ITEM: LOSS ON TERMINATION OF DISCONTINUED OPERATIONS
In December 1993 the directors decided to terminate the activities of the Pink Division and made a provision of £70,000 in the accounts for the year ended 31st December 1993 for the expected loss.

The loss on termination has decreased the group's tax charge for the current year by approximately £5,000.

INFALLIBLE LIMITED
NOTES TO THE CONSOLIDATED ACCOUNTS
FOR THE YEAR ENDED 31ST DECEMBER 1994

		1994 £000	1993 £000
5. **INTEREST PAYABLE LESS RECEIVABLE**			
Interest payable			
Bank loans and overdrafts and other loans			
wholly repayable within five years		67	152
Other loans, not so repayable		84	95
		151	247
Less: interest receivable		(7)	(4)
		144	243

Total interest payable and similar charges includes finance charges payable under finance leases and hire purchase contracts of £11,000 (1993: £6,000).

6. **PROFIT ON ORDINARY ACTIVITIES BEFORE TAXATION**
   After charging:

		1994	1993
Auditors' remuneration	– audit services	22	21
	– non audit services	14	8
Depreciation	– owned assets	49	45
	– assets held under finance leases and hire purchase contracts	89	42
Operating lease rentals	– plant and machinery	21	6
	– other	42	38
Profit on sale of fixed assets		(19)	(4)

The company has taken advantage of the legal dispensation allowing it not to publish a separate profit and loss account. The profit for the year after tax attributable to the parent company is £1,343,000 (1993 : £648,000).

7. **TAX ON PROFIT ON ORDINARY ACTIVITIES**

	1994	1993
Corporation tax based on the results for the year at a rate of 33%	669	375
Deferred taxation	43	(14)
	712	361

8. **DIVIDENDS**

	1994	1993
Interim dividend paid	50	50
Final dividend proposed	75	25
	125	75

INFALLIBLE LIMITED
NOTES TO THE CONSOLIDATED ACCOUNTS
FOR THE YEAR ENDED 31ST DECEMBER 1994

9. INTANGIBLE ASSETS	Group £000	Company £000
PATENTS AND TRADE MARKS		
Cost		
At 1st January 1994	23	6
Additions	221	221
Disposals	(9)	(9)
At 31st December 1994	235	218
Depreciation		
At 1st January 1994	9	1
Charge for the year	24	21
Disposals	(1)	(1)
At 31st December 1994	32	21
Net book value		
At 31st December 1994	203	197
At 31st December 1993	14	5

13

INFALLIBLE LIMITED
NOTES TO THE CONSOLIDATED ACCOUNTS
FOR THE YEAR ENDED 31ST DECEMBER 1994

10. TANGIBLE FIXED ASSETS GROUP AND COMPANY	Freehold land and buildings £000	Plant and machinery £000	Fixtures and equipment £000	Motor vehicles £000	Total £000
Cost or valuation					
At 1st January 1994	717	208	50	33	1,008
Additions	–	112	48	83	243
Surplus on revaluation	483	–	–	–	483
Disposals	–	(27)	–	(34)	(61)
At 31st December 1994	1,200	293	98	82	1,673
Depreciation					
At 1st January 1994	56	64	18	8	146
Charge for the year	13	61	13	27	114
Surplus on revaluation	(69)	–	–	–	(69)
Disposals	–	(18)	–	(8)	(26)
At 31st December 1994	–	107	31	27	165
Net book value					
At 31st December 1994	1,200	186	67	55	1,508
At 31st December 1993	661	144	32	25	862

The freehold land and buildings, which had previously been accounted for under the historical cost rules, were revalued on 31st December 1994 on an open market value basis by Gessit & Partners, chartered surveyors.

The historical cost and related depreciation of the freehold land and buildings is set out below:

	£000
Historical cost at 31st December 1994	717
Accumulated historical depreciation	(69)
Historical cost net book value at 31st December 1994	648

All other tangible fixed assets are stated under the historical rules.

The net book value of plant and machinery includes an amount of £180,000 (1993: £136,000) in respect of assets held under finance leases and hire-purchase contracts.

INFALLIBLE LIMITED
NOTES TO THE CONSOLIDATED ACCOUNTS
FOR THE YEAR ENDED 31ST DECEMBER 1994

11. INVESTMENTS

	1994 £000	1993 £000
Shares in subsidiary undertakings at cost	219	219

Details of group undertakings are as follows :

Name of company and country of incorporation	Description of shares held	Proportion held Direct	Indirect	Activity
Bertie Limited (England)	Ordinary shares	100%	–	Manufacture of colour designs
Cecil Limited (Scotland)	Ordinary shares	100%	–	Designers
Dellboy Limited (England)	Ordinary shares	–	75%	Distribution of colour designs

	1994 GROUP £000	1994 COMPANY £000	1993 GROUP £000	1993 COMPANY £000
12. STOCKS				
Raw materials and consumables	629	629	656	656
Work in progress	1,205	1,205	981	981
Finished goods and goods for resale	1,136	1,080	1,270	1,130
	2,970	2,914	2,907	2,767
13. DEBTORS – AMOUNTS FALLING DUE WITHIN ONE YEAR				
Trade debtors	3,243	2,699	2,382	2,025
Amounts owed by subsidiary undertakings	–	96	–	70
Advance corporation tax recoverable	–	–	8	8
Other debtors	173	173	140	140
Prepayments and accrued income	291	275	230	219
	3,707	3,243	2,760	2,462
14. INVESTMENTS				
Listed on The Stock Exchange at cost (Market value £43,000/1993: £36,000)	26	26	22	22

INFALLIBLE LIMITED
NOTES TO THE CONSOLIDATED ACCOUNTS
FOR THE YEAR ENDED 31ST DECEMBER 1994

15. CREDITORS – AMOUNTS FALLING DUE WITHIN ONE YEAR

| | 1994 | | 1993 | |
	GROUP	COMPANY	GROUP	COMPANY
	£000	£000	£000	£000
Debenture loan	90	90	90	90
Bank loans and overdrafts	448	448	870	870
Obligations under finance leases and				
hire purchase contracts	50	50	34	34
Trade creditors	1,942	1,895	1,581	1,554
Corporation tax	644	637	350	346
Advance corporation tax payable	22	22	8	8
Other taxation and social security	187	171	149	141
Other creditors	91	83	70	66
Accruals and deferred income	53	44	81	71
Proposed final dividend	75	75	25	25
	3,602	3,515	3,258	3,205

The bank loans and overdrafts are secured by a floating charge over the assets of the company.

16. CREDITORS – AMOUNTS FALLING DUE AFTER MORE THAN ONE YEAR GROUP AND COMPANY

| | 1994 | 1993 |
	£000	£000
Debenture loan	540	630
Bank loans and overdrafts due within five years	40	11
Obligations under finance leases and		
hire purchase contracts	127	79
	707	720

The debenture loan is repayable in equal annual instalments until 2000; £90,000 (1993: £180,000) falls due for payment more than five years from the balance sheet date; interest is $12^1/_2\%$ per annum; and the loan is secured by a floating charge over the assets of the company.

The bank loan is secured by a floating charge over the assets of the company.

The obligations under finance leases and hire purchase contracts are payable as follows:

| | 1994 | 1993 |
	£000	£000
Within two to five years	139	93
More than five years hence	54	21
	193	114
Less: Finance charges allocated to future periods	(66)	(35)
	127	79

INFALLIBLE LIMITED
NOTES TO THE CONSOLIDATED ACCOUNTS
FOR THE YEAR ENDED 31ST DECEMBER 1994

	1994	1993
17. PROVISIONS FOR LIABILITIES AND CHARGES	£000	£000
GROUP AND COMPANY		
Deferred taxation:		
Accelerated capital allowances	43	14
Other timing differences	–	(14)
	43	–
Less: advance corporation tax	(22)	–
Provision for loss on termination of discontinued operations	21	70
	(21)	70

As stated in Note 10, the company revalued its freehold land and buildings during the year. In the opinion of the directors, the revalued properties will be retained for use in the business and the likelihood of any taxation liability arising is therefore remote. Accordingly, the potential deferred taxation in respect of these properties has not been quantified.

	1994	1993
18. CALLED UP SHARE CAPITAL	£000	£000
Authorised:		
Ordinary shares of £1 each	100	100
Allotted, called up and fully paid :		
Ordinary shares of £1 each	50	50

19. CAPITAL COMMITMENTS		
Expenditure contracted but not provided for in the accounts	–	24
Approved by the directors but not yet contracted for	1,120	–

20. COMMITMENTS UNDER OPERATING LEASES
Payments which the company and group are
committed to make in the next twelve months
under non-cancellable operating leases:

	1994	1993
	£000	£000
Leases expiring within one year	10	10
Leases expiring between two and five years	54	38
Leases expiring more than five years hence	5	8
	69	56

21. CONTINGENT LIABILITIES

A customer has brought an action against the company, alleging faulty workmanship on a colour design. It has been estimated that the company's maximum liability, should the action be successful, is £80,000. The action is being vigorously defended and the company has been advised by Counsel that the action has little prospect of success. Accordingly no provision for any liability has been made in these accounts.

22. DIRECTORS' EMOLUMENTS

	1994	1993
	£000	£000
Aggregate emoluments:		
Fees	12	8
Management remuneration	179	149
	191	157
Emoluments excluding pension contributions :		
Chairman	50	47
Highest paid director	68	52
Other directors fell within the following ranges :	Number	Number
£5,001–£10,000	–	1
£10,001–£15,000	1	–
£35,001–£40,000	–	1
£40,001–£45,000	1	–

23. EMPLOYEE INFORMATION

Average number of people employed by the group (including directors) during the year:		
Production	124	122
Selling and distribution	80	81
Administration	54	49
	258	252
Costs in respect of these employees:	£000	£000
Wages and salaries	3,912	3,688
Social security costs	379	340
Other pension costs	249	228
	4,540	4,256

INFALLIBLE LIMITED
NOTES TO THE CONSOLIDATED ACCOUNTS
FOR THE YEAR ENDED 31ST DECEMBER 1994

24. PENSION COSTS

The contributions payable to the group's pension scheme are determined by a qualified actuary using the projected unit method.

The most recent actuarial valuation was at 31st December 1993. The assumptions which have the most significant effect on the results of the valuation are those relating to the rate of return on investments and the rate of increase in salaries and pensions. It was assumed that investment returns would be 7% per annum; salary increases would average 4% per annum; and that present and future pensions would increase at the rate of 3% per annum.

The valuation showed that the market value of the scheme's assets was £5,592,000 and that the actuarial value of those assets represented 104% of the benefits that had accrued to members, after allowing for expected future increases in earnings.

25. RECONCILIATION OF OPERATING PROFIT TO NET CASH INFLOWS FROM OPERATING ACTIVITIES	1994 £000	1993 £000
Group operating profit	2,333	1,291
Depreciation – tangible fixed assets	114	85
– intangible fixed assets	24	2
Profit on sale of tangible fixed assets	(19)	(4)
Debtors	(955)	(62)
Creditors	396	(67)
Stock	(63)	60
Net cash inflow from continuing operating activities	1,830	1,305
Net cash outflow from discontinued activities and reorganisation costs	(184)	(27)
Net cash inflow from operating activities	1,646	1,278

26. ANALYSIS OF CHANGES IN FINANCE DURING THE YEAR

Loans, debentures and finance leases:

Balance at 1st January 1994	844	1,009
Cash outflows from financing	(189)	(180)
Inception of finance lease contracts	192	15
Balance at 31st December 1994	847	844

27.

ANALYSIS OF CHANGES IN CASH AND CASH EQUIVALENTS DURING THE YEAR

Balance at 1st January 1994	(840)	(1,271)
Net inflow for the year	395	431
Balance at 31st December 1994	(445)	(840)

INFALLIBLE LIMITED
NOTES TO THE CONSOLIDATED ACCOUNTS
FOR THE YEAR ENDED 31ST DECEMBER 1994

28. ANALYSIS OF CASH AND CASH EQUIVALENTS SHOWN IN THE
BALANCE SHEET

	1994	1993	Change in year
	£000	£000	£000
Cash at bank	3	30	(27)
Bank overdraft	(448)	(870)	422
	(445)	(840)	395

Index